Emily Thursfield

England and Ireland

Emily Thursfield

England and Ireland

ISBN/EAN: 9783337322373

Printed in Europe, USA, Canada, Australia, Japan

Cover: Foto ©ninafisch / pixelio.de

More available books at **www.hansebooks.com**

HIGHWAYS OF HISTORY

ENGLAND AND IRELAND

BY

EMILY THURSFIELD

RIVINGTONS
WATERLOO PLACE, LONDON
MDCCCLXXXIV

CONTENTS

CHAP.		PAGE
I.	THE ANGLO-NORMAN KINGDOM IN IRELAND	9
II.	IRELAND IN TUDOR TIMES. THE WARS OF ELIZABETH	23
III.	THE PLANTATION OF ULSTER. THE WENTWORTH SCOURGE	53
IV.	THE CROMWELLIAN SETTLEMENT	67
V.	THE WARS OF WILLIAM III.	75
VI.	THE PENAL LAWS	84
VII.	THE VOLUNTEERS	102
VIII.	THE INDEPENDENT IRISH PARLIAMENT	109
IX.	THE REBELLION OF 1798. THE UNION	116
X.	IRELAND IN THE NINETEENTH CENTURY	125

CHAPTER I.

THE ANGLO-NORMAN KINGDOM IN IRELAND.

Introduction.—The two islands of Great Britain and Ireland are separated by a channel so narrow as to compel their political association, and yet so wide as always to have prevented their complete union. England was conquered by Rome, and received the impress of Roman civilization; but the Romans never attempted to gain a footing in Ireland. England became Protestant at the Reformation; Ireland remained Catholic. England has gradually acquired liberty by the constitutional progress of her people; the constitutional development of Ireland has been controlled and arrested by the jealousy of England. England has become commercial and industrial by the force of her natural resources and her geographical position; Ireland has remained almost wholly agricultural, partly because her mineral resources are inferior, partly because her efforts at domestic manufacture and foreign trade have in former times been sternly repressed by England.

Early Ireland.—Of ancient Ireland we know very little with certainty. Like Great Britain itself, Ireland was peopled by successive waves of Celtic immigration; but in the greater island invaders of Teutonic race have proved the stronger, and have overmastered and absorbed the Celts. In Ireland the contrary has taken place. All Teutonic invaders—the Ostmen, the Anglo-Normans, and the countless streams of English—have given way to the subtle Irish spell, and have either disappeared or put on a Celtic face. The phrase *ipsis Hibernis Hiberniores* has been applied from time immemorial to English settlers, and it indicates an important and abiding historical fact. Our chief concern is with the English in Ireland, but there are two points in the history of the early Irish which must be considered before we can rightly approach our subject. These are (1) The land system; (2) The system of the laws.

The Land System.—The early Irish lived in tribes or "septs," each headed by an elective chief. The method whereby the successive chiefs were elected was known as *Tanistry*. In the lifetime of the ruling chief the strongest or the most worthy adult member of his family was chosen to succeed him, and called the *Tanist*. The tribes held land, a great part of which was common and chiefly used for grazing, while part was appropriated to individuals.

The appropriated land was held on the tenure of *gavelkind;* that is, when a landowning member of a sept died its chief redistributed all the lands of the sept among the surviving households. The chief, as well as the other members of the tribe, possessed a private portion of land, but the chief had no rights over the common land; his authority was over the men of the tribe, but not over their land. This state of things was never quite understood by the English, and was the cause of much confusion and fighting. When the English first approached Ireland to conquer it the feudal system had taken firm root in England, and feudal ideas prevailed among the invading English. The characteristic feature of the feudal system was that all land had a lord, and that the lord granted lands to his vassals in return for certain services. From time to time, when the Irish chiefs submitted to their conquerors, the English king and his lords believed that the submission of the people and the surrender of the land followed as a matter of course. They attempted to deal with the land as in feudal England, and were startled when the common folk sprang up to claim it; it was as if the very clods dared to protest.

The Laws.—The ancient Irish laws are those known as the "Brehon" laws; that is, laws administered and interpreted by the "Brehons," or judges, one at least of whom was attached to each tribe. These laws had prevailed in the form of tradition and custom from time immemorial. In all criminal matters their underlying principle was compensation; a man paid an "eric"-fine, as it was called, of so many cows, according to the greatness of his crime; even a murderer only paid a fine. The Irish clung to these laws, but the English hated them; an English Act of Parliament called them "wicked and damnable." Yet the laws of our forefathers were very like these old Irish laws, which indeed embody only the ancient customs of all peoples of the Aryan race.

Introduction of Christianity, circa 432.—We have little authentic information as to the religion of the ancient Irish; but it seems to have been a form of Druidism, similar to that practised by the Celts of Gaul and Britain, and described by Cæsar. Christianity came to Ireland in the middle of the fifth century. Patrick, a youth of unknown country, was carried into Ireland as a slave; there he stayed for six years, but at last escaped, and went back to his home. It was the voice of God in a dream which called him again to the land of his captivity. He says: "In the dead of the night I saw a man coming to me as if from Hiberio, whose name was Victoricus, bearing innumerable epistles, and he gave me one of them, and I read the beginning of it, which contained the words, 'The voice of the Irish;' and while I was repeating the beginning of the epistle I imagined that I heard in my mind the voice of those who were near the wood Foclut, which is near the western sea, and thus they cried, 'We pray thee, O holy youth, to come and henceforth walk amongst us;' and I was greatly pricked in heart, and could read no more, and so I awoke." He journeyed all over Ireland, winning over first the chiefs, and then the clansmen, to the rage and despair of the Druids. He ordained many priests, and set them together in groups, which afterwards became monasteries. He also made many bishops; but these Irish bishops were not like the bishops of other countries. They had no districts to rule over, but roved about the world, preaching and teaching where they liked: they were much disliked by foreign bishops because of their interfering ways. Yet Irish missionaries did much good work, being men of great earnestness. The Irish schools of learning became very famous, and men came to them from all lands. The Irish Church was long very independent, and pursued ways of its own; but in the middle of the eleventh century St. Malachy, an Irishman and a friend of the great St. Bernard, tried to bring his native Church into union with and subjection to Rome, and to some extent he succeeded.

The Ostmen, circa 795.—At the end of the eighth century Ireland, like the rest of Western Europe, was invaded by Norsemen. The heathen host swarmed into the country, ravaging, burning, slaying, and carrying away captives. The invaders attacked with special fury the churches and monasteries, the monastery of Armagh being ten times destroyed and rebuilt. They settled down at the mouths of the great rivers, and built towns which grew and flourished, and traded with the towns of the Continent. From these towns they sallied forth upon the Irish, stirring up strife between the tribes, and oppressing them greatly. So there was constant fighting in the land between the Irish and their oppressors; but when two hundred years had passed the afflicted nation took heart, and led by King Brian, the greatest of the old Irish kings, rose up and fought fiercely against the strangers. Inch by inch the Irish king contested and won. What land he won he kept, and ruled over with a strong hand. His last fight was at Clontarf, by Dublin Bay. There, on Good Friday, in the year of our Lord 1014, "the last heathen viking, and the only king of Ireland, fell by each other's hands." For the century and a half that elapsed between "Brian's Battle" and the coming of Strongbow, Ireland was a chaos. The Church occasionally exercised a moderating influence for a time; but it was not powerful enough to effect a real union. No single tribe, and no individual ruler, succeeded as in England in establishing a permanent supremacy. It would be useless to chronicle these years of tribal war, the only effect of which was to pave the way for a new conqueror.

Description of Ireland.—Unlike most islands, Ireland is low in the centre and hilly round the edge. The central plain is of limestone, and is intersected by chains of lakes and wasted by acres of bog. The narrow seas which divide Ireland from England are comparatively shallow, but the west coast is worn and fretted by the deep Atlantic, from which rise the great mountains of primæval rock. All round the coast the mountains form a belt, save where the rivers push through, and in the south-west the river estuaries form very fine harbours. The climate is warm and very damp; the excessive moisture makes the harvest late, but gives Ireland splendid pastures. The boggy interior is little fitted for habitation; hence the chief towns are on the coast, especially the east coast, facing England. The division of Ireland into four provinces is of very ancient date, and belongs to tribal times; but the counties are of English make. Munster and Leinster were divided into twelve counties, much as they stand now, by John; Henry VIII. cut Westmeath out of Meath; Mary made King's County and Queen's County. The county divisions of Connaught and Ulster date from the reign of Elizabeth, though Antrim and Down are older.

The Anglo-Norman Conquest, 1170.—In the year 1170 the conquest of Ireland by the Anglo-Normans began. It had long been meditated. There was a theory of Christian sovereignty encouraged by Rome, and expressed in a Bull of Adrian IV., that "Ireland and all the other islands on which the light of the gospel of Christ has dawned . . . do of right belong and appertain to St. Peter and the holy Roman Church." Henry II. had sought and obtained from Pope Adrian IV., in 1155, permission "to enter the land of Ireland in order to subdue the people." But he had been busy with other matters, so Ireland had enjoyed a respite. At last Dermot MacMurrough, the elective chief or king of Leinster, who had for his crimes been driven out by his people, fled to Henry to beg for help. Henry, who was then in Aquitaine, was busy, as usual. He could not go to Ireland himself, yet he did not like to let slip the opportunity of beginning the work he had at heart; so he gave Dermot letters authorizing him to recruit adventurers throughout the Anglo-Norman dominions who should help him to recover his crown. In return for this grace Dermot did him homage, and this in the end caused strange confusion; for Dermot, the dispossessed chief, had no longer a shadow of right to his former sovereignty, yet he swore to Henry to hold the lands he professed to claim on terms of feudal service. Armed with the King's letter of recommendation Dermot proceeded to gather together a band of warlike adventurers. Richard de Clare, Earl of Pembroke, known as "Strongbow," agreed to join the force on condition that he should marry Dermot's daughter Eva, and succeed Dermot on his throne. This agreement, though entirely in accordance with the recognized principles of feudal tenure, was alien to the Irish tribal customs, which allowed no hereditary transmission of royal rights. Dermot made almost as strange an agreement with Robert Fitz-Stephen, the real leader of the expedition. This knight was the grandson of Nesta, the Princess of South Wales, whose numerous descendants are known as the "Geraldines." He persuaded most of his cousins to join in this enterprise. To one of them, Maurice Fitzgerald, and to Fitz-Stephen himself, Dermot granted the town of Wexford to be held in fee. As Wexford was in the hands of a Danish colony, the Geraldines had to conquer it for themselves. This they did, and settled down there, while Strongbow conquered Waterford, and married the Princess Eva. The Irish outside Leinster grew much alarmed at the success of the strangers. The clergy gathered together in trembling, and the Synod of Armagh solemnly declared that this evil had come upon the nation because Englishmen had been held in bondage. All the English slaves in Ireland were accordingly set free, yet the tide of conquest did not roll back.

Henry II.'s Jealousy of Strongbow.—Not only the Irish were alarmed; the English king began to fear, but for another reason. He saw Strongbow and the Geraldines forming in Ireland a Norman state for themselves, and he feared they might forget that he was their feudal lord, so he called their followers back to England, and prepared himself to head an army of invasion. Strongbow, whatever dreams he might have had of independent sovereignty, saw that he had no chance of freeing himself from the yoke of Henry II.; he sent a humble letter to the King, reminding him that it was by the royal leave he undertook the Irish business, and assuring his liege lord that what lands he had acquired he should hold at the King's free disposal. Henry delayed a while to answer this letter, and in the meantime Strongbow and his friends were assailed fiercely—first by the Danes of Dublin, and then by the native Irish, under King Roderic.

The Norman soldiers proved stronger than their enemies; Danes and Irish alike were routed and slain. Then came a letter from the King summoning Strongbow to England. At Gloucester a stormy interview took place between Henry II. and his over-powerful vassal, but in the end the King's wrath was appeased. Strongbow was pardoned on condition of giving up Dublin and the great ports to Henry II., and of holding the rest of his conquests in fee.

Henry II. goes to Ireland, 1172.—At last the King himself set out for Ireland, and landed at Waterford in October, 1172, with a great army and much pomp. The Irish chiefs did not attempt to resist, but flocked from all parts to his camp, and did homage. Henry marched in royal state to Dublin, and there entertained his new vassals, who were overawed by his splendour. Even Roderic, otherwise Rory O'Connor, the recognised King of Connaught, and in some sort overlord of the whole country, submitted humbly to the conqueror. But his submission, and that of the tribal chiefs, must not be taken too seriously. It was "their light submission only, wherewith in all ages they have mocked and abused the state of England." Henry won over the great Irish churchmen to his side, and then returned to England, having apparently secured his new conquest. He sent over his son John to rule Ireland, but John did not know how to govern, and his insolent ways angered the Irish. No sooner was the strong hand of Henry II. removed than the strife began again. Henry saw that his policy of conciliation towards the Irish chiefs was useless; he changed his tactics, and planned and executed stern measures of conquest. Only bearing in mind his former fears of

Strongbow's ambition, he worked not through the first settlers, but by new men, hoping to play them off one against the other, and so reign supreme himself.

The Political Settlement of Henry II.—Henry II. aimed at making Ireland the counterpart of England. He began to divide the land into counties; he gave charters to the chief towns; he appointed sheriffs and judges; he set up courts at Dublin. The Lord Deputy was made the chief person in the land, and he was helped by a council composed of judges, officers of state, and lords spiritual and temporal. Courts grew up as in England—Chancery, King's Bench, Common Pleas, and Exchequer. The Irish Parliament, when it was formed, in the last years of the thirteenth century, was but a greater council, to which more distant members were summoned. In 1295 knights of the shire were summoned; the burgesses probably did not make their appearance before the time of Edward III., being spoken of as summoned in 1341. An ordinance of 1359 speaks of the Commons as an essential part of Parliament. The earliest recorded statutes are of the year 1310, after which we possess none earlier than 1429, all intervening records having been lost.

Grants to the first Settlers.—Henry II. affected to plant the feudal system in Ireland, and under him and his successors all the land was parcelled out to Englishmen. These were the chief grants:

1. Meath, the old royal demesne of the overlord, was granted to Hugh de Lacy in 1172. De Lacy had to oust its Irish ruler before he could take possession. It afterwards passed into the female line, and vested in the Crown in the reign of Edward IV.

2. Leinster, claimed by Strongbow in right of his

wife, the Princess Eva, was confirmed to that earl by Henry II. It also passed into the female line, and was cut up, being divided among the five granddaughters of Strongbow.

3. Ulster was granted by Henry II. to John de Courcy. This earldom was afterwards regranted to Hugh de Lacy, passed by inheritance to the Earl of March, and finally vested in the Crown in the time of Edward IV.

4. Connaught was at the first assured to King Roderic and his heirs, of course on terms of feudal tenure; but, regardless of his promise, Henry gave up this province to Fitz Aldelm, and John, following in his father's footsteps, granted it to William de Burgo.

5. Cork and its surrounding territory being granted by Henry to Mylo de Cogan and Robert Fitz-Stephen, two of the Geraldines, remained in the hands of that great family.

These seignories were at different times erected into "counties palatine;" that is, their lords were like kings, holding courts and exercising sovereign power. So that Ireland was not ruled by one king, but by many: at one time there were nine of these independent princes. This state of things in itself would have been bad enough, but when we consider that these feudal lordships were superimposed on the Irish tribal organization, which was utterly disregarded, it is almost impossible to overrate the confusion.

Conflict of English and Irish Law.—The English law was administered (as well as might be, considering the divers jurisdictions) among the English in the land. The Irish were under their own old laws, the "Brehon" laws, and could not claim the king's justice. There were indeed five families who for some reason or other were admitted to the English laws. These were the O'Neils, O'Molaghlins, O'Connors, O'Briens, and M'Murroughs. They were known as "the five bloods." But the rest of the Irish were outside the law, though they often begged to be admitted within its pale.

The English Conquest of Ireland incomplete, and why.—Thus the Irish and the Anglo-Normans lived for a century and a half after the Conquest, keeping each other at arms' length and contending in vain and never-ending struggles; for this so-called Norman conquest of Ireland was unlike other conquests. The Normans did not exterminate the natives, as the white man is crushing out of existence the Red Indian of North America. They did not drive them into a territory apart and there keep them, as the English did to the Celts of Britain, whom they pushed into Wales and Cornwall. Nor, on the other hand, did they coalesce with them and become one people, as happened to the Normans and the English in England, and the Normans and Italians in the kingdom of Naples. The Irish, on their part, were never strong enough or united enough to rebel successfully to fling off the English yoke, nor were they submissive enough to bow to it except when held down by main force; so the struggle was hopeless. Let us try to find out why the battle was always drawn, and why the English did not make short work of it.

1. The colonists, not lying together in one district, but being scattered about, were not able to unite and show a firm front. They were moreover much given to quarrelling with each other and with the English

Government, and in these quarrels they made use of the Irish as allies.

2. The Norman armour and mode of fighting, so well adapted to the open plains and the pitched battles of France, were worse than useless in the woods and bogs where the Irish guerilla warfare was waged.

3. The colonists were not free to employ their resources in quelling the Irish; for the kings of England required from them money and men for other wars— English, Scotch, and foreign.

4. Absentee landlords were common then as now, and in their absence the native Irish clutched at their lands and kept them.

5. The settlers who did remain on their estates forgot that they were English, and took Irish names and lived in the Irish way. They intermarried with the Irish, and sent out their children to nurse in the families of their dependents, a custom known as fosterage, whereby the family relations both of the Irish themselves and of the English families settled in Ireland came, according to English notions, to be greatly confused. The English could not understand or allow that the same mother's milk might produce in Ireland the same close affections as common paternity produced in England. The system of "gossipred" or spiritual relationship, based on sponsorship, was equally unintelligible and equally distasteful to the English lawgivers, and attempts were made to discourage both fosterage and gossipred, as will be seen when we come to the period of the Statute of Kilkenny. The settlers employed Irish mercenaries to fight for them, quartering them out on the wretched people, and they let out their lands to Irish tenants; for the English did not find

it worth their while to be earth-tillers in the unsettled land.

6. The English population was to a certain extent fleeting. Mere adventurers would come over, seize land on some pretext, despoil and take to themselves what they could, then depart again across the sea, and this process was never-ending.

The Rebellion of Edward Bruce, 1315.—From the Anglo-Norman Conquest of Ireland to the beginning of the Tudor rule in 1534, the most noteworthy event is the rebellion of Edward Bruce, which is, as it were, a turning point. Up to that time, 1315, the English power and dominion seemed to be on the increase; but the structure was hollow, and collapsed under the blow of the Scotch invasion. Within fifty years after the death of Edward Bruce the policy of the English in Ireland became purely defensive, and from year to year their dominions decreased, tribal land reappearing, until at length the Pale, as the land subject to English jurisdiction was called, meant little more than Dublin.

At the beginning of the fourteenth century Robert the Bruce was King of Scotland, and looking round for ways to harass the English king, saw his opportunity in Ireland. He planned to set up his brother on the throne of that country. The Irish chiefs were as usual disaffected. They wrote to the Pope, John XXII., and in strong and outspoken terms set forth their miserable state of oppression, their hatred of their English tyrants, and their determination to rise for their freedom. They had asked Edward de Bruce, "brother german of the most illustrious Lord Robert," to lead them, and help them to get rid of the detestable yoke, and they sued for the Pope's sanction to their enterprise. The Pope did not answer this appeal, except by excommunicating all who took up arms with the Bruce against his "most dear son Edward, the illustrious King of England." Thus the rebellion began under the ban of the Church.

Edward Bruce landed, in May, 1315, at Carrickfergus, with a great army. He was met on the river Bann by a force under De Burgo, the "Red Earl" of Connaught and Ulster, which force he utterly defeated. Then he proceeded to take Dundalk and Carrickfergus, and to be crowned King of Ireland. King without a kingdom he set out to win the land. As in those days winter was not a time for fighting he rested awhile, and in the spring of 1316 marched southwards to meet the Deputy, whom he defeated at Ardscull, Kildare county; then he journeyed throughout Leinster victorious, fighting and destroying. In the spring of 1317 he held a regal court in the wasted land. His brother came over to help him, and the two going south strove to annihilate the English settlers.

The Story of John Clyn.—One John Clyn, a friar, tells this tale of their doings : " Item, in the same year (1316), about Christmas, arrived Lord Robert le Brus, who pretended to be king of the Scotch, passing across through the whole land of Ulster, where he landed, almost to Limerick, burning, slaying, plundering, sacking towns, castles, and even churches, going and returning." The Lord Robert, after this great march, went back to Scotland, leaving his brother to finish his own business. Then the English colonists gathered themselves together with a desperate resolve to oust the invader. They encamped at the mouth of a pass between Faughared and Dundalk, under Jean de Birmingham. They were far superior in numbers to the army of the Bruce, whose advisers were strongly opposed to an engagement. But the Scot, flushed with his eighteen victories, would not listen to prudence; he fought and fell, and his soldiers fled back into Scotland. But in his fall he shook the English kingdom in Ireland to its foundations. "He was slain," says Friar Clyn, "to the great joy and comfort of the whole kingdom in general; for there was not a better deed that redounded more to the good of the kingdom since the creation of the world, and since the banishment of the Finè Fomores out of this land, done in Ireland than the killing of Edward Bruce; for there reigned scarcity of victuals, breach of promises, ill performance of covenants, and the loss of men and women throughout the whole kingdom for the space of three years and a half that he bore sway, insomuch that men did commonly eat one another for want of sustenance during his time."

Decay of the Anglo-Norman State.—The Irish chiefs, seeing how feeble were the colonists to resist Edward Bruce, grew bolder and bolder, and began to win back the land. By degrees the English lands shrank up, and as they lessened the tribal occupation of land reappeared, and the face of things was again changed.

The Statute of Kilkenny, 1367.—Fifty years from the landing of Edward Bruce the famous Statute of Kilkenny was passed, which marked the abandonment of the scheme for conquering the whole island, and aimed only at ordering the ways of the English in Ireland who yet were loyal, and preserving them from the contamination of the mere Irish, and the degenerate

Anglo-Normans. This statute was passed in a parliament held at Kilkenny in 1367 by Lionel, Duke of Clarence, son of Edward III., titular Earl of Ulster and Lord-Lieutenant. By it the colonists were forbidden to wear the Irish dress, speak the Irish tongue, and ride bareback like the Irish. They were to have nothing to do with the Brehon law, nor with the practice called coyne and livery, of exacting from the people food and fodder for soldiers and their horses. They were forbidden to intermarry with the Irish; fosterage and gossipred were to be abandoned. Creditors were to claim their rights from the debtors alone, and not, after the Irish tribal custom, from all the family. The Irish bards, being often spies, were forbidden to come into the English land, and the colonists were ordered not to employ Irish mercenaries.

Law against Absentees, 1369.—In 1369 a law was passed ordering absentees to return to their estates on pain of forfeiting them to the Crown. These Acts were stringent in word, but in deed they were of no effect. The like had been enacted before, and have been enacted since, but the government in Ireland has rarely been strong enough to enforce them.

Richard II.'s View of Ireland.—The decay of the English kingdom in Ireland was very rapid. Richard II. thus speaks of the Ireland of his time. "In our land of Ireland there are three kinds of people—wild Irish our enemies, Irish rebels, and obedient English. To us and our Council it appears that the Irish rebels have rebelled in consequence of the injustice and grievances practised toward them, for which they have been afforded no redress, and that, if not wisely treated and given hope of grace, they will most likely ally themselves with our enemies."

The Irish enemies were ubiquitous and ceaselessly active; at every point they attacked the English land, and so fierce and active were they that in a very short space a great portion of it was again tribal land. The Irish rebels—as the original English settlers, degenerate through intermarriage and fosterage, were termed—were almost at one with the "enemies." "A very little more oppression and they would become enemies," said Richard II., and his prophecy was fulfilled. The obedient English might almost be counted; they included few besides the feeble lords of the Pale, and the three great earls—Kildare and Desmond (both Geraldines) and Ormond. These three earls were virtually independent and were much more powerful than the Government, which they only occasionally condescended to recognise. The Desmond was almost an Irishman in habit and feeling, and his cousin of Kildare only one degree less. The earls of Ormond, whose vassals dwelt in Kilkenny and Tipperary, were the most civilized and faithful supporters of the Government. But on this account they had far less power in the land than the Geraldines.

The weak English Government struggled on, though the lack of an army prevented it from really accomplishing its work of repelling the Irish, and of keeping in order the few loyal subjects left. Instead of cherishing this remnant the Government continually harassed it with demands for men and money to carry on useless raids in the enemy's country. Some sort of order might have been obtained if the great earls had been allowed to act as independent princes, but this was prevented by the jealousy of the Government, which, far from strengthening the earls, stirred up and encouraged strife between them and the chiefs, in order that none should be strong enough to overset its weak and tottering edifice. The last years of the fourteenth century are full of the attacks of the Irish chiefs, and the black mail paid by the English.

Richard II.'s doings in Ireland, 1395-1399.— In 1395 Richard II. landed at Waterford with a great army. He marched with some difficulty along the coast to Dublin, and summoned the Irish chiefs to meet him. The more crafty ones, knowing that the King's force was too strong for them, gathered together, seventy-five in all, among them MacMurrough, O'Brien, O'Connor, and even The O'Neil, and did homage. "With these humilities," says the chronicler, "they satisfied the young King, and by their bowing and bending avoided the present storm, and so brake that army which was purposed to break them." The King once over the sea again, the "trick and imposture" was revealed. "Those Irish lords laid aside their masks of humility, and, scorning the weak force which the King had left behind him, began to infest the borders, in defence whereof the Lord Roger Mortimer, being then the King's lieutenant and heir-apparent of the crown of England, was slain. . . . Whereupon the King, being moved with a just appetite of revenge, came over again in person, in the twenty-second year of his reign, with as potent an army as he had done before, with a full purpose to make a full conquest of Ireland." The purpose was not fulfilled. Wandering about in the hill country between Waterford and Dublin, "his great army was much distressed for want of victuals and carriage," and he accomplished nothing. Then came the news of Bolingbroke's landing at Ravenspur, and the unlucky King hastened back to England, "where shortly he rendered both his reign and his life."

The Brotherhood of St. George, 1480.—The English land in Ireland during the fifteenth century was of small extent, being parts only of the counties of Dublin, Meath, Kildare, and Louth. The colonists flocked back to England in such numbers that an Act was passed to thrust them back into Ireland again. What colonists remained disliked the restrictions of the Statute of Kilkenny, and constantly asked for and obtained licenses to evade it. The Pale was in a wretched state, being constantly oppressed and pillaged. It was walled round with a strong wall, and this for a time was a protection to the unhappy colonists. The Government was entirely powerless to keep order; an Act was passed empowering the colonists themselves to seize and kill all marauders or intending marauders. Accordingly the English formed themselves into an armed defensive band, called the Brotherhood of St. George. Thirteen gentlemen from the four English counties chose a captain, and supplied 120 archers, 40 horsemen, and 40 pages. This constituted the armed force of England in the land. The Parliament, which in the palmy days of the Anglo-Norman state met with tolerable regularity, and did a fair amount of business, dwindled into a mere assembly of the Pale; the three great earls and all distant folk got leave to absent themselves because of the extreme difficulty of travelling through the "enemy's" country.

Ireland and the Wars of the Roses.—Ireland was involved to a certain extent in the wars of the Roses.

Richard, Duke of York, was sent over as Deputy in the reign of Henry VI., to be out of the way. He became very popular. Exiled from England, and attainted in 1459 after the battle of Bloreheath, he returned to Ireland, and made himself Deputy again. The Irish Parliament warmly supported him, and took the opportunity of stoutly asserting its independence of the Parliament of England. Many Irish lords followed the Duke back to England, and died fighting for the White Rose. The Yorkist pretenders all found friends in Ireland, and the displeasure of Henry VII. rested on the colonists. He bound the Irish Parliament with a chain, which fettered it for three centuries; this was Poynings' law.

Poynings' Law, 1494.—This celebrated Act, named from the Deputy of the time, Sir Edward Poynings, so runs: "No Parliament be holden hereafter in the said land (of Ireland), but at such season as the king's lieutenant and council there first do certify the king, under the great seal of that land, the causes and considerations, and all such acts as to them seemeth should pass in this same Parliament; and such causes, considerations and acts affirmed by the king and his council, to be good and expedient for that land, and his license thereupon, as well in affirmation of the said causes and acts, as to summon the said Parliament under his great seal of England had and obtained. That done, a Parliament to be had and holden after this form and effect before rehearsed; and if any Parliament be holden in that land hereafter, contrary to the form and provision aforesaid, it be deemed void and of none effect in law." At the same time it was enacted, as Bacon says, that "all the statutes of

England were made to be of force in Ireland; for before they were not, neither are any now of force in Ireland which were made in England since that time." The chief castles were at the same time placed in the hands of Englishmen, and a determined effort was made to govern by means of English officials.

Ireland for the Irish, 1496.—This utterly failed, and the King then adopted the opposite course, and attempted to rule Ireland through the most turbulent of the Irish. The doubtful story of the royal saying illustrates a certain fact. The Bishop of Meath, rehearsing in the King's ear the enormities of the Earl of Kildare, wound up by saying that all Ireland could not rule this earl. Whereupon the King replied, "Then in good faith shall the Earl rule all Ireland." At any rate the Geraldines became virtual kings in Ireland, and ruled until 1534, when a fresh change was wrought in the conduct of Irish affairs.

CHAPTER II.

IRELAND IN TUDOR TIMES. THE WARS OF ELIZABETH.

The Power of the Geraldines begins to wane.—
Henry VIII. for many years attempted to rule Ireland by "sober ways, politic drifts, and amiable persuasions, founded on law and reason;" but by repeated experience he found out that these were not the ways of the Geraldines, and he began to be stern with those unruly lords. Thrice was the Earl of Kildare summoned to London to answer for his sins—his trafficking with the Irish enemies. On his first visit he appeared at court, married the Lady Elizabeth Grey, and triumphantly returned to Ireland as Lord-Deputy. Obeying the second summons, he was thrown into the Tower; but he freed himself by craft and returned to his office. On his third visit he was again thrown into the Tower, and gravely charged outright with treason. This led to the downfall of the Geraldines.

The Silken Lord's Rebellion, 1534.—By a trick they were forced into rebellion. Kildare had left his son, "Silken Thomas," as Vice-Deputy. A report was spread in Dublin that the Earl had been executed, whereupon his son in rage determined to fling off his allegiance to the English. He raised the standard of revolt, and the armed followers of the Geraldines flooded the Pale. The English were prompt to respond; an army under Skeffington landed. This force was strengthened by a train of artillery. The artillery carried the day, and the castles of the rebels were soon battered down. Silken Thomas surrendered and was sent to the Tower, but not to join his father; for the old Earl died of grief at his son's mishaps. Five more Geraldines were treacherously captured and sent also to the Tower. A year afterwards they and the Silken Lord were hanged at Tyburn. There remained a child-heir to the noble house, and he was carried to Rome, where, under the care of Cardinal Pole, he was brought up to be no faithful subject of England, as Elizabeth found out.

Lord L. Grey Deputy, 1536.—The strong Tudor hand was making itself felt. Lord Leonard Grey, brother of the Marquis of Dorset, and brother-in-law of the Earl of Kildare, was made Deputy. He was an active and resolute man and a tried soldier. His first work was to quell the west, which was up in arms under the Earl of Desmond and O'Brien, the self-styled Prince of Thomond, the pest of the South by reason of his bridge. "O'Breene's Bridge," a massive structure, protected by two castles, one "very strong, builded all of hewn marble," spanned the Shannon at Castle Connell, and was the highway by which the wild chieftain overran Munster at his will.

He takes O'Brien's Bridge, 1537.—Lord Leonard, after one or two small successes, attacked this bridge. For a whole day his gunners assailed it, but in vain, so strong was it. Then the soldiers, forsaking the use of artillery, by sheer courage and strength scaled and stormed the bridge, and the Irish fled. The mayor and aldermen of Limerick came out in great joy to see the dreaded bridge. They crowded on it, and curiously examined the castles. Then the work of the big guns showed itself; the bridge cracked and fell, and the city worthies were plunged into the river, to be ignominiously fished out. Lord Leonard wished to follow after O'Brien and dare him to fight in his own country, but money failed him, and his soldiers flatly declined to go further without pay. They condescended to take a neighbouring castle; then the Deputy returned dispirited to Dublin, to enter into hopeless and bitter struggles with his council.

His Downfall, 1539.—Influenced by his relations with the Geraldines, Lord Leonard conceived a hatred for their hereditary foe, the Earl of Ormond, and grew dangerously Irish in his sentiments. Throughout the land the enemies of England were stealthily forming themselves into a league. The primary object of this confederation was to restore to his inheritance of Kildare the young Gerald Fitzgerald, Cardinal Pole's pupil; but it speedily grew bolder, and with foreign aid planned to crown the representative of the house of O'Neil King of Ireland on Tara Hill. Desmond "began the dance," but the clash of arms aroused Lord Leonard from his dream of treason. He went into the field, and, defeating The O'Neil, broke for the present the prospects of the league. Then, the King being made acquainted with his doubtful loyalty, he was flung into the Tower on charge of treason. He pleaded guilty, and was beheaded.

Sir A. St. Leger Deputy, 1540.—Sir Anthony St. Leger, a wise and prudent man, succeeded as Deputy. In his time Ireland was comparatively at peace. The

Irish chiefs, as well as the Norman-Irish nobles, sat in his Parliaments, and were gladdened by the gifts of the Church lands, in return for which in 1541 they made Henry VIII. king of Ireland. His ancestors had only been styled lords of the island.

Act of Supremacy passed in Ireland, 1537.—The Church lands had not been surrendered to Henry VIII. without a struggle. The Reformation, so-called, began in Ireland in the year 1537, when, in a Parliament called by Lord Leonard Grey, the Act of Supremacy had been passed, the mouths of the procters, or clerical members of the Parliament, having first been stopped. In the same Parliament appeals to Rome were forbidden, first-fruits were allotted to the King, and certain abbeys were suppressed. Five years later the remaining religious establishments fell, all the forfeited lands became the property of the Crown, and Henry VIII. granted them to those whom he wished to propitiate. For the last five years of his reign the Irish were quiet, under the rule of St. Leger.

Ireland under Edward VI., 1547–1553.—But no sooner was Henry VIII. dead than strife began again, with the new element of religious animosity embittering the warfare. "If the Lords of the Council," sighed a later Deputy, "had letten all things alone in the order King Henry left them, and meddled not to alter religion, the hurley-burleys had not happened." St. Leger's gentle hand was unavailing in this new state of things; he was replaced by Sir Edward Bellingham, one of the most remarkable rulers ever sent to Ireland.

Sir Edward Bellingham Lord Justice, 1548.—He made his strong hand felt during his two years' rule in

Ireland, and none dared to lift their voices against him in any dispute religious or agrarian. But unluckily he died, and the disorder returned. St. Leger came over again, and, by orders of Cranmer and the Earl of Northumberland, brought with him the new service book of the English Church, which he attempted to bring into use, with but little success. St. Leger was much troubled by the captains whom he found in command: they endeavoured to continue the stern rule of Sir Edward Bellingham, and this did not suit the mild ways of St. Leger.

The Currency Troubles.—Money matters too were a great trouble to this Deputy; he could get no money from the Home Government, and the Irish mints, by a bad device of the English Council, issued only base money, which the Irish despised. St. Leger was recalled, and Sir James Crofts succeeded him.

Sir James Crofts Lord Justice, 1551.—The new ruler, distressed at the misery caused by the base money, entreated that its manufacture should cease, and that what "silvered brass" had already been issued should be depreciated to its true value. The English Council declared that they saw no necessity for such action, and bade Crofts devote himself to planting in Ireland the Christian—that is the Protestant—religion; then would all troubles cease. The Deputy clung to his own opinion, and held a council of trade in Dublin, which, after long discussion, concluded that there was no remedy for the public distress but to reduce the value of the base money, and addressed an earnest entreaty to that effect to the English Council. For some time longer nothing was done until the enormous rise in prices brought "slaughter, famine, and all kinds of misery."

At length Northumberland gave way, the base coin was reduced, and bought in, and new was issued.

Mary, 1553.—A little quiet came to Ireland with the accession of Mary. Her views about religion suited her Irish subjects; under her Gerald Fitzgerald was restored to his earldom of Kildare.

Elizabeth, 1558.—Elizabeth for the first eighteen months of her reign avoided Irish affairs, till the rebellion of Shan O'Neil called for her attention.

Shan O'Neil rises in Rebellion, 1559.—The province of Ulster contained two great and strong families, both claiming to be royal—the O'Neils and the O'Donnells. The O'Neils were descended from the ancient overlords of Ireland, and in general triumphed over their rivals; but the O'Donnells during the reign of Mary had made great headway, having become closely allied to the Scots of the western isles, who had settled in thousands on the coasts of Antrim and Down. The Irish O'Donnells and the Scotch M'Connells alike had to bend before Shan O'Neil. He was the son of Con O'Neil, one of the chiefs who had surrendered their tribal lands to Henry VIII., to receive them back on terms of feudal tenure. Con received from the King the title of Earl of Tyrone, and he chose as his heir one of his illegitimate sons, Matthew Kelly, who took the title of Baron of Dungannon. This angered the lawful heir Shan, who caused the baron's death, though whether by craft or in open warfare is uncertain. He then deposed his father and drove him out into the Pale, and, despising the English title, got himself elected chief in the old tribal way. He set aside the son of the murdered baron, and with his foot on the stone was proclaimed "The O'Neil." Shan lorded it in Ulster, but his ambition looked further afield than his native province. During the absence of the Deputy, Lord Sussex, in England, Sir William Fitzwilliam was in command, and certain tidings of widespread disaffection reached him. Shan, the Geraldines, and O'Brien of Inchiquin, were all in secret league against the English Government, and only waited for help from France and Spain to rebel openly. Foreign help failed, and the southern earls returned to their allegiance; but Shan stood somewhat aloof, and his mind could not be known. He was summoned to England to explain to Elizabeth his action with regard to his father's possessions, though his deeper plots were ignored in the summons. He affirmed his utmost willingness and even his eager desire to appear before the Queen; he wrote a letter to her himself, saying that nothing hindered him from starting but the lack of money. He asked for a loan of £3,000 in English money, promising to repay the Queen in the base Irish money. He asked also for a safe-conduct, and for an English wife, and many other favours. A long correspondence between Shan and the Government in Dublin ensued, and Sussex, now again at his post, gathered troops and secured allies to attack the troublesome chief. The Deputy himself and the Earl of Kildare were to move up from the south, O'Donnell was to swoop down from the north-west, and the Hebridean Scots were to close in on Shan from the east; thus was the great rebel to be surrounded and overthrown. But this plan was not to be carried out. Before the allies had time to attack Shan was upon them. He captured O'Donnell and his wife, and through the influence of the captive lady, who was the Earl of Argyle's sister, he gained the

Scots to his side. The Deputy, bereft of his northern allies, advanced with the forces of the Pale strengthened from England, and invaded Ulster, only to be utterly defeated and disheartened. Then Lord Sussex shamefully trafficked with one Neil Gray and with Shan's seneschal, to induce them to murder the proud rebel; but the plan was not carried out, as Shan discovered it. Some desultory fighting took place, but at length a peace was patched up, a safe-conduct was given to The O'Neil, and money for his journey was sent.

He goes to England, 1561.—Then he set out for England to make his submission to the Queen. The submission was duly made on the 6th of January, 1652, and the Queen forthwith began to indulge in the craft so dear to her. Shan's safe-conduct stated that he should be allowed to return to Ireland, but fixed no limit to his stay in England. Elizabeth and her advisers meant to keep him at court till his affairs should be settled according to their will. He demanded to be recognized as his father's heir, and was told that his case must be fully considered before English judges, and that his nephew and rival, the young Baron of Dungannon, must come over and state his own claim, that all things might be done in order. The young baron was ostensibly sent for, but private orders reached Fitzwilliam not to allow him to leave Ireland. The winter passed away, and nothing definite was done. Shan constantly appealed to the Queen to confirm him in his father's earldom, promising on his side to uphold her power throughout all Ulster. His professions of loyalty did not, however, prevent him from intriguing with the Spanish ambassador. As the baron did not appear, Shan grew alarmed, and determined to free himself from the net of the English Queen. He tried with all his Irish wit and flattery to persuade Elizabeth to set him free, but the honeyed words were of no avail; the Queen would not let him go. Then news came that the boy Baron of Dungannon was murdered by "the bank of a deep river" in the North. There was no evidence to connect Shan with the murder, yet it happened at a strangely lucky time.

He returns to Ireland, 1562.—It was hard to delay the acknowledgment of Shan as heir to his father's possessions when no rival barred the way. The baffled Queen let him go almost on his own terms. He promised indeed to take the oath of allegiance before the Deputy; but oaths to him had little meaning. He was styled Captain of Tyrone, and allowed to exercise feudal jurisdiction over the northern counties. A wider range than the northern province was opened to his power. He was permitted to call upon the Deputy to fight for him against any chief or lord who wronged him. If the Deputy failed to take action in twenty days Shan might raise an army and fight himself. A small pretext sufficed' to start him in his old career of fighting. He invaded Tyrconnel, "killing, robbing, and burning in the old style," with a view to force the O'Donnells to submit to him. The Deputy, casting about in his mind how to deal with this terrible captain, for the second time betook himself to treachery. He summoned Shan to meet him at Dundalk in order to swear allegiance, and sent him a safe-conduct so craftily worded as to leave him the power of arresting The O'Neil. Shan, however, suspected treachery, and stayed away, whereupon complaints of his obstinacy were sent to England. A third trap was then laid for

Shan by Sussex. The Deputy had with him in Dublin a fair sister. Shan, who had not succeeded in carrying off a wife from the English court, thought that this lady might suit him, and sent proposals to Sussex, who in return invited Shan to come to Dublin and make acquaintance with the lady, but The O'Neil would not. "He had advertisement out of the Pale that the lady was brought over only to entrap him, and if he came to the Deputy he should never return."

Fighting began again, but the Deputy met with no success. Shan lorded it in Ulster, harrying the lands of all who dared to oppose him. He was on the high road to establish himself as supreme over the "Irishry" in all the land; he was plotting with the Pope, the Spaniard, and the Queen of Scots. Sussex tried hard to stand out against the rebel, but his troops mutinied for want of pay, and he had not "one penny of money." In default of any other course of action Elizabeth made peace with Shan on his own terms. By the new treaty he became virtually king in Ulster. The first result of the peace was another attempt on his life. Poisoned wine was sent to him as a present from Dublin; he and his household drank of it, and only escaped death because the poison was not strong enough. There was no evidence to prove Sussex guilty of the murderous attempt. One John Smith of Dublin had sent the wine, and was severely reproved for the deed. He could not by law (as interpreted at the time) be punished by death, as the crime, to which he confessed, had not been completed. He might have been imprisoned; but it was thought that Shan would derive no satisfaction from so mild a punishment, and

THE WARS OF ELIZABETH. 33

so the matter dropped, Smith going free. Recovered from the deadly wine, Shan ruled in Ulster, "the only strong man in Ireland." Ulster was too narrow for his ambition. Before long he ranged over Connaught, demanding "the tribute due of owld time to them that were kings in that realm." It was plainly seen that either Shan or the English Government in Ireland must fall.

Sir Henry Sidney is sent over, 1566.—Sir Henry Sidney was sent over to make an end of the Irish wolf. On his landing the new Deputy summoned Shan to meet him at Dundalk, but The O'Neil refused to come. Messengers then passed between Sidney and the rebel, but the end of all negotiation was, that Shan stoutly declared that what he had won by the sword he would keep by the sword. The sword then remained the last and only appeal. Sidney's plan of attack was comprehensive. Shan had assailed and dispossessed of their land all the Ulster chiefs who had refused to acknowledge him as their lord. These chiefs were to be reinstated, and to form so many centres of opposition. Harassed in his own land of Ulster, O'Neil was to be attacked at once from the north and the south by a force encamping at Derry and by an army from the Pale. Shan, with all his wit and power, could not stand against this organized attack. He appealed to France for help, but in vain. No foreign aid came to him, and one by one his native allies deserted him.

Shan's Downfall and Death, 1567.—His last battle was fought with the ancient enemies of his house, the O'Donnells, who had joined with the Deputy. It was near Londonderry, on the west side of the river which runs into Lough Foyle. The O'Donnells were inferior

D

in numbers, but the fortune of war was theirs. Panic seized the O'Neils; they fled before their enemies, and the river received those who escaped the sword, so that scarce a man remained alive. Shan himself was not among the slain; he fled for his life to the far north of Antrim, and took refuge with the M'Connells. Three days afterwards he was slain in a brawl by the fierce Scots, his enemies of old. "His head," reported the Deputy, "sundered from his body, was . . . carried into the city of Dublin, where it was bodied with a stake, and standeth on the top of your Majesty's Castle of Dublin."

After the death of the great rebel a blow was dealt at his family. The very name of O'Neil was declared to be extinguished, while Tyrone, and Shan's other lands in Ulster, were declared to be forfeit to the crown. Nevertheless Turlough Luineach O'Neil assumed the headship of his clan, and, notwithstanding his direct disobedience to so recent an enactment, Elizabeth made a treaty with him on January 20th, 1570.

The Pope's Bull of Excommunication, 1569.—Two years after the death of Shan O'Neil, Pope Pius V. issued a Bull excommunicating Elizabeth and depriving her of her throne. This Bull had a disastrous effect on Ireland; for the English Government naturally thought that the Irish people, being Catholics, would do their utmost to dethrone the heretic Queen denounced by the Holy Father. Stern measures were, therefore, carried out in Ireland; the Anglicising policy was in full swing. To exterminate the native Irish, and to replace them by new English settlers, appeared to Elizabeth's advisers to be the best course of action; hence the wretched attempts of Sir Thomas Smith and the Earl of Essex in the North, hence the Desmond rebellion and the planting of the South. To the hatred of the Irish for the English was now added the hatred of the Catholic for the Protestant, and the despairing rage of the landowner about to be despoiled. The agrarian grievance was old, the religious grievance new; but from this time the two were entwined, and became hard to separate.

Sir Thomas Smith and the Earl of Essex.—Two attempts were made to plant English and Protestant colonies in the North of Ireland. One was planned in 1572, by Sir Thomas Smith, and conducted by his son; this utterly failed. The other and more famous failure is connected with the name of Walter Devereux, Earl of Essex. His idea was to expel the Hebridean Scots from the coasts of Antrim, and to plant the vacant land with Englishmen, leaving the interior to Irish tenants, who were to be under his sway, as well as their English neighbours. The Queen made him a grant of "that part of Ulster called Chandeboy," with extraordinary powers to do as he liked, even "power to make slaves and to chain to ships and galleys all or any such of the Irishry or Scots-Irish as should be condemned of treason, for the better furtherance of his enterprise." In August, 1573, the "enterprise" was begun. Elizabeth had begged Essex to "win the Irish by mildness." In furtherance of the royal wish the Earl began by some sort of negotiation with Sir Brian MacPhelim, an Ulster chief. Mild ways were, however, soon at an end. Sir Brian, seeing that the invading army was not very large, joined with The O'Neil and the Scots, and began to resist Essex. The English Earl managed to win over to his side the tribes who resisted the supremacy of The O'Neil, and there was fighting up and down Ulster, wasting of the land and terrible slaughter.

The Massacre at Raghlin, July, 1575.—Part of the Earl's plan was to dispossess the Scots who had settled on the Antrim coast. These Scots naturally resisted. Their chief Surleyboy entreated that he and his men might remain in the homes they had made for themselves, swearing to be faithful servants of the Queen. Essex paid no heed to Surleyboy's messages until he had made an end, with much "killing," of the Irish opposition. Then he gave a terrible answer to the Scottish chief. The island of Raghlin, rocky and difficult to approach, lies off the Antrim coast, near the Giants' Causeway. This island the Scots had fortified, and thither, as to a refuge, they sent their wives and children. Essex sent his soldiers to attack the island, and they made short work of the task. They speedily destroyed the fortifications, and then put to death, not only the armed men who had opposed them, but all the women and children who were hidden about in the caves and rocks of the island. "Surleyboy himself," says Essex, in a letter to the Queen, "stood upon the mainland of the Glynnes and saw the taking of the island, and was likely to have run mad for sorrow, tearing and tormenting himself, and saying that he there lost all that ever he had." Notwithstanding this and other cruel and unscrupulous deeds of Essex in the North, his "enterprise" did not succeed. He got into difficulties with the Queen about money matters, the Irish Government would afford him no help, he lost heart, sickened in a mysterious way, and died in Dublin, September 22, 1576.

THE WARS OF ELIZABETH.

The Presidents.—The southern province was harried in a like manner to the northern. The attempt to Anglicise was nowhere successful. A device long meditated by Elizabeth's advisers was carried into execution. Presidents were appointed in Ulster, Munster, and Connaught, who should act as sub-Deputies, and enforce the English law.

Act to reduce all Ireland to Shire Land, 1569.—In 1569 an Act was passed, making all Ireland into shire land. This virtually did away with the Brehon law, and deprived the chiefs of their ancient privileges. The land being planned out in the English fashion tempted fresh English adventurers, who were bitterly opposed by the Irish.

Sir Thomas Stukely, 1578.—The troubles in the South were encouraged by emissaries of the Jesuits. In 1578 one Sir Thomas Stukely, a wild and disreputable adventurer, who had been a pirate and a friend of Shan O'Neil, set out from Civita Vecchia with a force gathered together by the Pope to oust the government of the heretic Queen from Ireland. Stukely met on the way a Portuguese force bound for Morocco, and changing his mind forgot Ireland, joined the Portuguese fleet, and perished in the adventure.

Sir James Fitzmaurice at Smerwick, 1579.—The next year brought an ill-fated force to Ireland. Nicolas Sanders, ex-Papal Legate, and Sir James Fitzmaurice, accompanied by a motley crew of priests and laymen of various nationalities, scarce a hundred in all, landed in Dingle harbour, in Kerry, with much pomp, bringing with them a Papal Bull and a consecrated banner. They meant to conquer the land by means of the Irish army, which they expected to flock to their standard.

The army was slow to gather, and the handful of adventurers built a fort at Smerwick on "a very small neck of land, joined to the shore by a bank of sand," a situation which did no credit to their strategy. Fitzmaurice tried to get the Earl of Desmond to join him, hoping so to win over the vast Geraldine following to that visionary army. Desmond wavered, being uncertain which would profit him most, rebellion or loyalty; but two of his brothers joined Fitzmaurice, and with them many others of the clan, and the rebel army began to grow. The government woke to a sense of danger, and Sir Nicholas Malby took the field with a few hundred English soldiers, and with the Burkes of Connemara and Mayo, who were at feud with the Geraldines. A fight took place in the wood of Limerick, and Fitzmaurice was killed. This defeat was a great blow to the rebels, and Sir William Drury, the Lord Justice, set out on a march to finish the business. But he was in feeble health, and wandering with his troops in the great wood of Limerick to find the enemy he grew bewildered, and the Irish set upon his forces and discomfited them. He died shortly afterwards.

The Desmond Rebellion, 1579.—Then Desmond took the field, and all the men of the South rose up in arms, drawn by their allegiance to the Geraldine and cajoled by the promise of help from Spain. Massacre and plunder marked the path of the rebels through Munster. Violent and cruel as were the ways of the insurgents, they were met by equal violence and cruelty on the part of the Queen's forces. Elizabeth sent over the Duke of Ormond to be military governor of Munster, and expected him to reduce the province to order. It was thought that the fact of the chief insurgent being his hereditary foe would urge him on. Burghley wrote to him by the Queen's orders, and thus ended his letter : " So now I will merely say Butler aboo, against all that cry in a new language Papa aboo, and God send you your heart's desire to banish and vanquish those cankered Desmonds." The "cankered Desmonds" were to be overthrown by an orderly plan, carried out with steady and terrible exactitude. A fleet, under Sir William Winter, sailed to the coast of Kerry to support the land forces. Sir William Pelham, the new Lord-Deputy, and Ormond, each with a small force, set out at the same time, the one from Dublin, the other from Kilkenny, with the intent to meet near Limerick. Pelham himself tells in a few words the story of their doings. " We passed," he says, " through the rebel countries, consuming with fire all habitations, and executing the people wherever we found them." Working on in the same thorough fashion, the English generals, after the junction of their forces, proceeded to attack the strong castle of Carrigafoyle. With the aid of artillery they carried it ; then one stronghold after another fell before them. Pelham went near to capture Desmond, his wife, and the Legate, in the Castle of the Island, in Kerry ; but they escaped him and fled into the wilds. The Englishmen only turned in their march of destruction when they reached the Atlantic, at the edge of Kerry ; then they returned to Cork. In that year of grace, 1580, Ormond says that he put to death " eighty-eight captains and leaders, with 1547 notorious traitors and malefactors, and above 4000 others." There was a great quiet in the crushed province. Winter, acting on his own responsibility, and believing that all danger was over, took the fleet home.

The Spaniards land at Smerwick, 1580.—Then, the coast being clear, came the long-promised foreign help —800 Italians and Spaniards, sent by the Pope, with a great store of arms for the Irish. Some of them went inland in search of Desmond; the greater number entrenched themselves in the deserted fort of Smerwick.

Risings in the Pale, 1580.—At the same time a rebellion broke out in the Pale, which had long smarted under illegal exactions. At its head was James Eustace, Lord Baltinglass, an ardent Catholic, who was joined by Sir John of Desmond and his men. A new Deputy came to deal with this rising, the Lord Grey de Wilton, whose first act brought upon him a disastrous defeat. The rebels of the Pale lay in Glenmalure, a narrow valley in the mountains. Up this gorge the Lord-Deputy sent his men, himself standing at its mouth. The English soldiers marched well into the narrow pass. When they had reached the heart of it, of a sudden armed men started up on every side and assailed them. There was no escape, and they were shot down like dogs. Some thought that Kildare, who stood with the Deputy at the mouth of the gorge, had given warning to his countrymen. Lord Grey gathered himself together, and with a small force, including among others Edmund Spenser and Walter Raleigh, left the Pale and marched to the south-west to Smerwick. Ormond, as military governor of Munster, had appeared on the scene with 4000 of his men soon after the arrival of the foreigners; but he only looked at the little fort and went away again.

Massacre at Smerwick, 1580.—Lord Grey, on his arrival before Smerwick, had to wait till Winter came back with the fleet. Then the siege began, and lasted for three days, at the end of which time the besieged, finding that they could hold out no longer, begged for terms. Lord Grey would grant no terms to men sent by the Pope, "that detestable shaveling," as he called him. He demanded unconditional surrender, and the unlucky strangers had no choice but to give way. The general, Don Bastian de San Josepho, and his officers, came out with ensigns trailing, and gave themselves up. They were put to ransom, but the common men, in number six hundred, were slaughtered, and laid out on the sand, "as gallant and goodly personages as ever were beheld," said the Deputy. The English captains looked upon their death as a necessary example, and it may be that they were right.

Suppression of the Rebellion, 1582.—The Papal force was thus disposed of in a manner not calculated to encourage the despatch of any more foreign troops to Ireland. The Desmonds and the Legate were still wandering in the wilds, but Lord Grey returned to the Pale, and speedily made short work of the rebels there. Kildare was arrested on suspicion, and presently taken to London, where, three years afterwards, he died in the Tower. The Wicklow rebels were hunted from their fastnesses; all the disaffected, high and low, were accused of treason, convicted, and hanged. In the South, Ormond as governor, Raleigh and others as captains, were busy hunting out the last rebels, the followers of the Desmond. Sir John and Sir James of Desmond were caught and killed; the aged Legate, unused to privation, died of hunger and cold; but the Desmond still lived, and till he was got rid of the work could not be considered at an end. He was hunted from place to place, and at last, one morning in October, 1583, some English soldiers found him and killed him. His body was swung up in Cork, and his head spiked on London Bridge. With him ended the great Desmond rebellion.

The Desolation of Munster.—The province of Munster lay almost emptied of people, a fact scarcely to be wondered at when the manner of warfare, described by Pelham himself, is considered. Writing to the Queen, he says: "Touching my manner of proceeding, it is thus: I give the rebels no breath to relieve themselves, but by one of your garrisons or the other they be continually hunted. I keep them from their harvest, and have taken great preys of cattle from them, by which it seemeth the poor people, that lived only upon labour, and fed by their milch cows, are so distressed as they follow their goods, and offer themselves, with their wives and children, rather to be slain by the army than to suffer the famine that now beginneth to pinch them."

Spenser's description of Munster.—It was purposed to confiscate the land of the rebels and plant it with English settlers. The land indeed was in woeful plight. Edmund Spenser, who was among the settlers, thus describes its state: "Notwithstanding that Munster was a most rich and plentiful country, full of corn and cattle, that you would have thought they should have been able to stand long, yet ere one year and one-half they were brought to such wretchedness as that any stony heart would have rued the same. Out of every corner of the woods and glens they came, creeping forth upon their hands; for their legs could not bear them. They looked like anatomies of death; they spoke like ghosts crying out of their graves; they did eat the dead carrions, happy where they could find them; yea, and one another soon after, inasmuch as the very carcases they spared not to scrape out of their graves; and if they found a plot of watercresses or shamrocks, there they thronged as to a feast for the time, yet not able long to continue there withal; that in short space there were none almost left, and a most populous and plentiful country suddenly left void of man and beast; yet, sure in all that war there perished not many by the sword, but all by the extremity of famine, which they themselves had wrought."

Plantation of Munster, 1586.—It was planned to colonise the land wrenched from these wretched people under the direction of Sir John Perrot, Deputy in succession to Lord Grey de Wilton. He first held a Parliament and passed two Acts of Attainder against the rebels—Desmond, Lord Baltinglass, and all the lesser men. By these acts the lands of the attainted became Crown property. The confiscated lands were divided into seigniories of 12,000, 8,000, 6,000, and 4,000 acres each, to be held in fee of the Crown at a nominal rent, with great privileges attached. Among the "undertakers"—so the new settlers were called— were Walter Raleigh and Edmund Spenser. One of the chief conditions on which these grants were made was that no Irish were to be admitted as tenants. This condition was naturally set at nought. The English farmers and labourers who were needed to make the plantation a success did not find their new venture attractive; they were continually plagued by the native Irish, who formed themselves into secret societies. So they returned to England as fast as they could, and the new landlords were obliged to take on the old tenants, there being no others to be had.

Sir John Perrot Deputy, 1584.—Sir John Perrot was Lord-Deputy from 1584 to 1588. He was a just man, and his policy towards the Irish was on the whole one of conciliation. Among the English settlers in Ireland he had many enemies, for he had a bad temper, and was imperious towards those under him. Talebearers carried mischievous stories of him to the Queen; he fell into disgrace, was recalled, and died in the Tower. His departure was a disaster for Ireland; for his successor, Sir William Fitzwilliam, was unwise, inconsiderate, and arbitrary. He irritated and oppressed the Irish, and in his time the English soldiers throughout the land behaved with such violence and insolence that disaffection was general, and the outraged people could not but rebel. This, the last and greatest rebellion of Elizabeth's reign, was headed by Hugh O'Neil, Earl of Tyrone.

Early Life of Hugh O'Neil, Earl of Tyrone.—Hugh O'Neil was the son of the Baron of Dungannon, murdered by Shan O'Neil in 1558, and the younger brother of the boy baron who was slain while Shan was in London. He had been brought over to England by Sir Henry Sidney, educated at Court in the English fashion, and was the English candidate, so to speak, for power in Ulster, as opposed to Turlough Luineach, self-styled The O'Neil. He was a very able man, and as he had been nurtured under English influence the Government hoped to use him, and the influence of his great name, in the work of winning Ireland over to English ways. He was an officer in the Queen's army, was accounted a loyal subject, and was greatly in favour with Elizabeth. He was stationed on the borders of Ulster, and began his career in his hereditary lands by fighting on every occasion and pretext with his kinsman—The O'Neil. Holding fast to the English side, he gradually got the better of Turlough. In 1584 he gained a portion of Tyrone; three years later the rest of the territory belonging to the ancient earldom was granted to him, together with the title of Earl of Tyrone. His zeal grew with his possessions. In 1590 he entered into communication with the Government as to the ordering of Ulster, offering to do all in his power to bring the province into English ways, and affirming, not for the first time, that the name of The O'Neil ought to be suppressed. The Government gladly availed themselves of his help, and he continued fighting with his old kinsman. The Deputy speaks of "a great controversy between the Earl and Sir Turlough O'Neale, by reason of a fray fallen between them, in which the dutiful old knight, Sir Turlough O'Neale, was shot through the shoulder with a bullet, and stricken with a horseman's staff in the small of the back—two grievous wounds, but (God I thank) will recover. I sent him a surgeon with a great deal of stuff for his dressing." Sir Turlough was growing old, and had not strength and energy to carry on hostilities with his kinsman Hugh. He retired from the fray, stipulating only for certain lands and money.

Tyrone Rebels, 1595.—Tyrone was no sooner left the richest and strongest O'Neil than his loyalty and his love of English rule and order disappeared. The high hopes which the Government had founded upon him sank, and the disaffected Irish chieftains plucked up heart. There was a great prospect of success for a rising, headed by one of the ancient royal house, especially such a one as Hugh, Earl of Tyrone.

It was some time before open war broke out. Disputes were rife between Tyrone and the Dublin executive. A new Lord-Deputy, Sir William Russell, was sent over, and to the surprise of all Tyrone hastened to Dublin, and made submission on August 13th, 1594. Secret instructions from the Queen reached Russell, ordering him to detain Tyrone; but the Deputy disobeyed these instructions, and was bitterly reproached for his behaviour. By slow degrees Tyrone prepared for action. His mock submission smoothed things outwardly for a time, and he began to build up a confederacy against the power of England. His first wife had been an O'Donnell, and through her he had formed a friendship with her brother, Red Hugh, a determined enemy of England. The two great houses of O'Neil and O'Donnell found no difficulty in rallying round them the greater number of the Ulster lords; and many chiefs in the other provinces. The religious cry was raised; an appeal was made to the rancour of the Catholic against the heretic; finally, Tyrone made supplication to the Spanish king for help.

Tyrone's war began in a very desultory fashion. The native forces in Ulster amounted to about 17,000 men, being about three times as great as the entire forces of the Queen in Ireland. Numbers, however, do not represent the true state of the case. Tyrone could not depend on his great force keeping together or acting in concert for any length of time; he therefore confined himself to harassing the English soldiers and drawing them into small encounters. He was waiting until help should come from Spain, or until Elizabeth should be worried into making peace with him on his own terms. The latter contingency happened. The Queen, fretted by the continual and ineffectual warfare, and not recognizing how deep the canker of rebellion had eaten into the heart of the land, determined to make peace. She wished to break up the league by separately reducing each chief to submission; but Tyrone was as yet too strong for her. He would not let his fellow-rebels out of his net; he was their spokesman in all negotiations. He dragged out the correspondence, expecting always the help of Spain; but he firmly adhered to his demand that liberty of conscience should be granted to his countrymen, and that no English garrisons should be stationed in lands belonging to Irishmen. The first point was not much pressed, being chiefly raised as a matter of form; but to the second Tyrone clung with deadly tenacity. The English recognized its importance, and would not yield upon it. The negotiation dragged on, and Tyrone claimed to act for all the insurgents throughout the land. Elizabeth was forced to acknowledge the widespread character of the league. She would not yield to the demands of the insurgents, she could not stifle them; she therefore went on writing letters. The rebels throughout the land took heart, seeing how slow to act was the Government. There was great hope among the Irish, and great fear among the English. "There is no part (of Ulster) freed from the poison of this great rebellion," says a contemporary writer, "and no country, or chieftain of a country, whom the capital traitor Tyrone hath not corrupted and drawn into combination with him." "This great rebellion" pressed hard upon the small English force in Ireland. There was a lack of food among the soldiers stationed in the North, and Sir

Henry Bagnal, the Lord-Marshal, whose sister Tyrone had abducted, marched with several thousand men to relieve the famine-threatened garrisons.

Battle of the Yellow Ford, 1598.—On his way from Armagh to Portmore, as Blackwater Town was then called, Sir Henry Bagnal fell in with the Irish army on August 15th, 1598, and a battle took place, in which the English were utterly defeated; Bagnal himself was slain with thirteen of his officers, and 1500 of his soldiers and all the arms and provisions were captured. Those soldiers who escaped with their lives fled away, and the English army of the North ceased to exist. Fynes Morrison, a contemporary writer, says: "The English, from their first arrival in the kingdom, never had received so great an overthrow as this. Tyrone was among the Irish celebrated as the deliverer of his countrymen from thraldom; and the general voice of Tyrone among the English after the defeat of the Blackwater was as that of Hannibal among the Romans after the battle of Cannæ." This great defeat was quickly followed by risings in every quarter. The English strongholds in the North surrendered, and Ulster fell into rebel hands. All Ireland indeed was suddenly wrested from her conquerors, except Dublin and a few other towns; for once the Irish were almost united.

Lord Essex arrives, 1599.—But the temporary union of the Irish chieftains could not long avail against the power of England and her armies. Lord Essex, son of the ill-fated Walter Devereux, came over, in April, 1599, with twenty thousand men, commanded by veteran officers. Against this, the greatest army ever sent to Ireland by Elizabeth, what could the undisciplined forces of the rebels effect? Tyrone did all in his power to avoid a pitched battle; he was waiting for the promised assistance of Spain. Lord Essex had no great success, however. He made an expedition into Munster, in the course of which he was much harassed, and lost many men. The Queen was angry with him for wasting his time and losing his men in the South; she sent him more soldiers, and he marched northwards into Ulster, but there was no fighting. He had an interview with Tyrone, and the two leaders agreed to an armistice. Then Essex hurried back to London to explain to the Queen Tyrone's views and his own actions. How he fared belongs to English history. As regards Ireland, the only results of his efforts were the waste of a year, and the loss of several thousand men.

Lord Mountjoy Deputy, 1600. — Charles Blount, Lord Mountjoy, came over as Lord-Deputy in 1600. He at once began to reform the army on strict religious principles, thus anticipating the celebrated new model of Cromwell. He also adopted a mode of warfare more effectual than the hasty raids of his predecessors. He sent forces to the various strongholds, from which they were to harry the country, speedily returning again to their refuge. This strategy steadily pursued was gradually successful. The North and the South were most obstinate in holding out. Sir George Carew, President of Munster, worked well in his province, and took the strongholds by degrees; and even in Ulster, Tyrone's own land, many forts were held by the English. Tyrone himself, and Red Hugh, his brother-in-law, still bore arms, and still avoided battle, whilst they waited for the aid of Spain. At length it came, five years after it had been promised.

Arrival of the Spaniards, 1601.—In the autumn of 1601 a Spanish veteran force of 3500 men landed at Kinsale. Their leader, Don Juan de Aquila, immediately put forth a declaration to the people, wherein he said: "We, commiserating the condition of the Catholics here, have left our most sweet and happy country, Spain, that is replenished with all good things; and being stirred with their cries, which pierce the hearers, having reached to the ears of the Pope and our good King Philip (III.), they have (being moved with pity) at last resolved to send into you soldiers, silver, gold, and arms, with a most liberal hand, not to the end they might (according as they feign) exercise cruelty towards you, O Irish Catholics, but that you may be happily reduced (being snatched out of the jaws of the devil, and freed from their tyranny into your own pristine ingenuity), and that you may freely profess the Catholic faith. Therefore, my most beloved, . . . the Pope, Christ's vicar on earth, doth command you to take arms for the defence of your faith. I admonish, exhort, and beseech you all . . . that as soon as possibly you can you come to us with your friends and weapons. Whosoever shall do this shall find us prepared, and we will communicate unto them those things which we possess; and whosoever shall (despising our wholesome council) do otherwise, and remain in the obedience of the English, we will persecute him as an heretic, and a hateful enemy of the Church, even unto death."

Battle of Kinsale, 1601.—To the dismay of Don Juan the Irish did not respond to his invitation; he expected an army to gather round him, but not a man appeared. Then he fell back upon the hope of O'Neil joining him; but all the might of England was put forth to prevent this junction. Three days after the Spaniards had landed an English force sat down before Kinsale; a week later the Deputy and Sir George Carew arrived. Reinforcements poured in, and presently the town of Kinsale was closely blocked on every side; no way was left open by which O'Neil could reach the Spaniards. For two months the siege was carried on, both Spaniards and Englishmen suffering. Tyrone and Red Hugh with their army marched towards Kinsale. Sir George Carew left the besieging force, and tried to stop them; but the rebels, through their better knowledge of the country, eluded him, and managed to join a new foreign force of about 1000, which had just landed. Many of the Munster chiefs rose and joined The O'Neil, who then took up his position north of the besieging army and waited. From the 8th of December until the 23rd the armies waited; neither would strike the first blow. Then Tyrone suddenly made up his mind, and on Christmas-eve, 1601, he led his men to the attack, hoping to surprise the English. Hastily as his resolution had been made, there was yet time for one of his men to betray him. The Irish found the enemy ready for them, and more than a match for them. Fortune speedily declared herself for the English, and the rebel army broke and rushed away in a despairing flight. The unlucky Spaniards, deserted by those whom they had come to succour, surrendered. The vessels which had brought them returned to Spain bearing many of the Irish who fled from their own land—among them Hugh O'Donnell, who went on a fruitless errand to beg for more help, and died in Spain.

Tyrone Surrenders, 1603.—O'Neil now returned to Ulster, and the Deputy, after a march of destruction through Cork and Kerry, betook himself to the North, and there wrought such fearful havoc that Tyrone, realising the utter hopelessness of his enterprise, surrendered absolutely on the 25th of March, 1603. On the same day Queen Elizabeth died.

CHAPTER III.

THE PLANTATION OF ULSTER. THE WENTWORTH SCOURGE.

The Vanquished Land.—Mountjoy's terrible plan had succeeded. The Irish who remained after Elizabeth's last wars lifted up their heads and beheld their fruitful land barren. The crops had been destroyed. The English general had done this work deliberately, meaning to starve the people. There was no food in Ireland, and there was no money wherewith to buy foreign food, for the base money which the Queen had sent to her Irish subjects was useless for such a purpose. The wretched Irish wandered up and down the country in search of food. They devoured docks and nettles and other weeds, and the English soldiers found them lying dead with ghastly green faces. Gangs of women entrapped and ate little children, and Sir Arthur Chichester with his own eyes saw three little children devouring their dead mother. Starvation and such loathsome food brought pestilence, and the people perished by thousands of the famine and the plague.

English Ways come in.—Now was the time, thought James I. and his advisers, to break the spirit and tame the pride of these insolent islanders. Irish ways were to disappear; Ireland was to be made like England. The Brehon laws, so often derided and contemned, were to disappear; the system of land tenure was to be assimilated to that of England; the Irish tongue and Irish customs were to go. Justice was to be administered as in England; the judges were to go on circuit, the King's writ was to run throughout the land.

Religious Reform attempted, 1605.—In religion also Ireland was to follow her mistress. The Irish Catholics, having regard to certain tendencies of James while he was only king of Scotland, began to hope, after his accession to the English throne, that they would be allowed liberty of worship. They were mistaken. The new King showed himself much more stern and unyielding in this matter than his predecessor. On the 4th of July, 1605, he issued a proclamation ordering all persons in Ireland to attend church, and banishing all priests.. Then began a wearisome and hopeless struggle between the Deputy and the recusants. Sir Arthur Chichester, who had succeeded to the office of Deputy in the autumn of 1604, was an active and energetic man, and fitted to be a ruler in virtue of his wisdom and knowledge of men. Wise to plan, and prompt to carry out, he yet recognised the limits set to him by the nature and will of those with whom he dealt, and his instinct led him to stop at the right point. Believing that things would never go well in Ireland until the Irish followed the State Church humbly and willingly, he pursued at first a stern and vigorous course towards the recusants. The shilling fine imposed by law for each absence from church was enforced. This, thought Chichester, did not press hardly enough on the well-to-do, whose action was important as influencing the lower orders. He therefore constituted the Castle Chamber a kind of spiritual tribunal, before which he summoned rich and important recusants, who were imprisoned or heavily fined. A short trial of such measures showed the Deputy that they were useless to effect his object, and hurtful in many ways. He gave up attempting to coerce the recusants, and began to think that to educate the young in the religion of the State was the right way to deal with the religious difficulty in Ireland. As he said: "In these matters of bringing men to church I have dealt as tenderly as I might, knowing well that men's consciences must be won and persuaded by time, conference, and instructions, which the aged here will hardly admit, and therefore our hopes must be in the education of the youth; and yet we must labour daily, otherwise all will turn to barbarous ignorance and contempt. I am not violent therein, albeit I wish reformation, and will study and endeavour it all I may, which I think sorts better with His Majesty's ends than to deal with violence and like a Puritan in this kind." The wise Deputy accordingly betook himself to the task of reforming the weak and wretched Protestant Church, so as to make its fold more inviting to the erring Papists.

The Flight of the Earls, 1607.—Civil as well as religious reform was needed. Ulster claimed much attention. It was impossible for that province to live quietly after the English mode while O'Neil and O'Donnell lorded it there. It is true that the representatives of those two ancient royal houses—Hugh O'Neil, Elizabeth's rebel, and Rory O'Donnell—masked under the titles of Earl of Tyrone and Earl of Tyrconnel, were attempting to forget their ancient state, and to live as English subjects. But for them this was difficult, and for the English and official Irish it was very trying to see the late rebels held in honour. One of the latter says: "I have lived to see that damnable rebel Tyrone brought to England, honoured and well liked. Oh, what is there that does not prove the inconstancy of worldly matters? How I did labour for all that knave's destruction! I adventured perils by sea and land, was near starving, eat horseflesh in Munster, and all to quell that man, who now smileth in peace at those who did hazard their lives to destroy him; and now doth Tyrone dare us, old commanders, with his presence and protection." Whether Tyrone was really in earnest or not in his endeavour to be loyal he was not credited with sincerity. His life was made a burden to him by reason of spies and suspicion, and Tyrconnel was in no better case. In May, 1607, a terror arose in Dublin. A paper was dropped at the door of the Council Chamber by an unknown hand. This paper, vaguely worded, gave information of a plot to murder Chichester and seize on the government. Tyrone's name was mentioned. There was nothing worthy the name of evidence to connect him with this plot, if plot there was. But he was called to account; the King himself decided to investigate the matter in London. Tyrone began to prepare for the journey, which he never accomplished. He received a warning from abroad that danger awaited him in London. The friend who sent the warning sent also an armed ship, and in that ship Tyrone and Tyrconnel, with all their belongings, fled from Ireland, never to return. Their flight marked them as guilty in the eyes of the world; the Government attainted them, and rejoiced in the opportunity of gaining such great and fair lands as theirs by confiscation.

THE PLANTATION OF ULSTER. 57

The Plantation of Ulster Planned.—The attainder of the two Earls seemed to the government of James I. to offer a favourable opportunity for attempting to secure the loyalty of Ulster by a new plantation, as it was called. This plantation of Ulster was founded on a gross injustice. It was assumed by the Commissioners that the lands confiscated—the counties of Tyrone, Donegal, Coleraine, Armagh, Fermanagh, and Cavan—were the freeholds of the attainted Earls, and that they might, therefore, be appropriated by the Government. In fact, however, the absent lords had, whether by old Irish custom or by new English law, absolute possession only of their own private estates. They had only certain rights of lordship over the tribal lands at large, which were the common property of all the members of the tribe. These humble commoners, many thousands in number, were nevertheless looked upon as mere tenants-at-will, and their rights were accordingly disregarded by those who planned the plantation.

The Views of Chichester disregarded.—Had Sir Arthur Chichester been heeded this would not have been. He knew Ireland and her ways better than any man of his time. He made a survey of the land to be planted and drew up an account of it, which he handed to the Commissioners on October 14th, 1608. He strongly urged that lands should be first given to the native Irish, then to the servitors (or retired officials, civil and military), and last of all to the undertakers (or English and Scotch colonists); but the Commissioners would not listen to the Deputy. They drew up a scheme of their own, which differed from Chichester's in the vital matter of the rights of the Irish commoners. The natives were first to be dispossessed; then the plantation was to proceed as should seem fit to the Commissioners. The chief among them was Sir John Davis, the able but unscrupulous Attorney-General. His view of the matter, as opposed to Chichester's, was unfortunately supported by Lord Bacon in a treatise which the latter drew up and presented to the King. The Deputy had the unwelcome task of carrying out the plantation on lines of which he disapproved. Two things had led, it was thought, to the failure of the Munster plantation. The estates granted were of too great extent, and the English settlers were exposed to the contaminating influence of the Irish. These errors were to be avoided in Ulster, where no portion was to exceed 2000 acres, and whence the Irish, with very few exceptions, were to be driven out.

The Irish attempt to Resist.—The unlucky Irish made one despairing attempt to keep their homes. They got down a lawyer from the Pale, who urged on their behalf the King's promise to protect the possessions of all his loyal subjects. The Dublin lawyer was no match for Sir John Davis, who affirmed that the Irish held their lands by no titles which could be recognized in law, and that, therefore, the declaration did not apply to them. The luckless people held their peace, and slowly and reluctantly dragged themselves away from their homes to the pitiful holdings provided for them.

The Plantation is accomplished.—The settlers made their appearance, and their wealth and energy changed the face of the country. The city of London took up Coleraine and rebuilt Derry, which was from that time called Londonderry. Manufactures began to grow, and Ulster made vast strides in material prosperity. One provision of the Commissioners was not carried out.

They had attempted to exclude the Irish from the lands of the undertakers, but the attempt was as usual unsuccessful. None knew so well as the Irish the nature of the country and its ways; the dispossessed tenants were kept on as humble dependents of the settlers and mere labourers, and the practice was winked at. Moreover, many of the English and Scotch who became tenants under the settlers did not like their position, and there were always natives at hand ready to pay all they could scrape together for the privilege of occupying their own land again. This was the beginning of the so-called Ulster tenant-right. The result of the plantation of Ulster may thus be summed up. The province acquired a large and loyal population of English and Scotch Protestants, whose wealth enriched and beautified the land. But underneath the wealthy and contented settlers groaned the wronged and despoiled Irish, only restrained from open rebellion by the double garrison which the Deputy was forced to post, though he cursed the Commissioners in his heart. "They know not Ireland so well as I do," he sighed. The year 1641 showed who was right.

Beginning of Protestant Ascendancy.—The Ulster Plantation, by providing a population who would send loyal and Protestant members to represent them in Parliament, was the real beginning of the period of Protestant ascendancy in Ireland. In the Parliament of 1613, by jugglery and corruption, a working majority, composed of men alien in religion and sympathy from the majority of the nation, was returned to act as the tool of the government. A disgraceful conflict as to the election of a Speaker marked the opening of this Parliament. When the Deputy ordered that a Speaker should be chosen the majority chose the ever-ready Sir John Davis; while the Roman Catholics, enraged at finding themselves in a minority, not only chose Sir John Everard, one of themselves, but placed him bodily in the chair. To the Protestants no better course appeared than to thrust Sir John Davis down on to the lap of Everard, and a most unbecoming scuffle ensued. The Protestants carried the day; Everard was unseated; his supporters retired from the House in dudgeon, and the whole case was referred to the King, who seized the opportunity of delivering a lecture, comprehensive and inconsequent, as was his wont, to his subjects of the Irish Parliament. The upshot of it all was that Sir John Davis retained the Speakership, and under his guidance the Parliament proceeded to carry out the king's wishes. The statutes prohibiting intercourse between the English and the Irish were all repealed, and free liberty of intercourse between all classes permitted and encouraged, the purpose being to weld all the dwellers in Ireland into one nation. The formal attainder for treason of Tyrone, Tyrconnel, and others was passed; and last of all a subsidy was granted, and an appearance of peace was secured by a general pardon and act of oblivion.

Plantations in Leinster, 1612-24.—Parts of Leinster were planted in the same manner as Ulster; but as no convenient flight of landowners had occurred, the King had to seek other means of obtaining the land. Doubts were raised as to the rights of the Leinster Irish to their lands, and a "commission to inquire into defective titles" was sent by the King. The Commissioners, having before them so excellent an example as Sir John Davis, were soon able to come to a decision pleasing

THE PLANTATION OF ULSTER. 61

to the King. It was held that large portions of land in Leitrim, Longford, Westmeath, King's County, Queen's County, Wicklow, and Wexford, having been granted to colonists some centuries before in early Plantagenet times, had in theory reverted to the Crown by death, flight, or surrender, though in reality they had been seized upon by certain presumptuous Irish. These, notwithstanding their centuries of occupation, were now to be ousted, in favour of the King, the rightful owner of the property. This iniquitous judgment was carried out. Thousands of Irish were driven out, some into the unprofitable lands in the immediate neighbourhood, others into the wild west.

The O'Byrnes.—The fate of the O'Byrnes of Wicklow is typical of the worst English ways of the time. Their territory was needed, but the pretext of a royal title could not be alleged; for both Elizabeth and James had given orders that the title of the O'Byrnes should be recognised as valid. Accordingly Sir William Parsons and other agents of the King falsely accused the O'Byrnes on a vague charge of treason. To sustain the charge false witnesses were suborned. Witnesses who proved restive were tortured, one being placed naked on a burning gridiron. The O'Byrnes in the end escaped, but not with their lands.

Projected Planting of Connaught, 1624.—Connaught now remained the only unplanted province of Ireland, and greedy eyes were cast upon it, wild and waste land as it was. Schemes were laid by the government, and a trick was devised whereby the titles of the Connaught landowners were pronounced to be defective. The Crown stepped in and claimed the lands, and a plantation was planned. The men of Connaught, fearing the fate of the men of Ulster, prepared to pay blackmail to the king. They offered to double the annual tax which they had paid since the time of Sir John Perrot, and also to pay the King a fine of £10,000 if only they might be confirmed in their possessions. The offer proved tempting to the needy King, but he had not time to close with it before he died, in 1625.

The Graces, 1626.—Charles I., soon after his accession, was confronted by an earnest petition from his Irish subjects for the relief of their grievances, civil and religious. They asked from him certain "graces," over fifty in number, of which the most important were : That sixty years' possession of land should ensure the owner against resumption by the Crown; that the lords, gentlemen, and freeholders of Connaught and Clare, should be admitted to enrol the surrenders made in the last reign, and should be confirmed in their estates; that an Act should be passed for a general pardon; that certain grievous monopolies should be revoked or limited; that the soldiers should be restrained from oppression in levying taxes; that the Castle Chamber—a tribunal accused of oppression—should be restricted in its jurisdiction; that certain gross abuses in the Church should be reformed; that Roman Catholic lawyers and others should be dispensed from taking the Oath of Supremacy, and should be allowed to take a new Oath of Allegiance, the wording of which did not offend their consciences. In return for these graces the Irish agreed to pay £120,000 to the King, who gladly closed with this bargain. More than one-third of the subsidy was paid into the treasury; but, unhappily, history affords no evidence of the fulfilment of the King's part of the compact.

Wentworth comes as Deputy, 1633.—Ireland, with the "graces" dangling before her, was now to undergo a period of despotism. The famous Thomas Wentworth, afterwards Lord Strafford, was sent over as Deputy, being a man after the King's heart. Wentworth did not believe in parliamentary institutions, or in the capacity of the many to govern. He thought the absolutism of the few more conducive to order, and he came to Ireland to set up absolutism, and to train up an Irish army in implicit obedience to himself and to the King, so that it might at some future time be useful in subduing the sturdy English. He set himself to pursue his objects with a firm purpose and an ungracious manner. His first care was to show all men that he meant to be master; his second, to remodel and improve the army, which was wretchedly inefficient; his third, to get money for his work.

Wentworth's Parliaments, 1634.—Wentworth announced that he intended to hold two parliaments— one in the summer, and one in the winter; the former to obtain the necessary supplies, the latter to enact as many of the graces as he thought desirable. The first, the King's Parliament, was carefully packed and astutely handled. Judiciously playing off Protestants against Catholics, the Deputy succeeded in getting liberal supplies. The second, the People's Parliament, met on the 4th of November, 1634, and transacted certain business deemed necessary by the Deputy. The matter of the graces Lord Wentworth lightly passed over as of little moment. He adroitly explained to the obsequious Parliament that many of the articles among the graces demanded by the Irish were only temporary expedients for which the need had now passed away, that others were meeter to be trusted to the honourable care of the subordinate officers of the Government, many more to his own honour and justice. Some few he passed into acts; but in two points the Deputy thought fit to deny the request of the Commons—the limitation of the King's title to sixty years backwards, and the confirmation of the landowners of Connaught in their estates. As these two points were the most important of all, Wentworth's refusal to entertain them was practically a rejection of the "graces," and a breach of the compact for which the King had already received a substantial consideration.

Wentworth deals with the Irish Church. — The Church of Ireland was at this time in a deplorable condition. Not only had poverty and ancient oppression disfigured the Church, but it appeared to Wentworth that the demon of dissent was clutching at those who should have been gathered into her fold. Throughout the length and breadth of the land were obstinate Roman Catholics, and in the North were the Scotch settlers, sturdy in their Presbyterianism. Wentworth set out to reform all things, with the help and advice of his friend Laud. He sternly restored all temporalities which he considered to have been stolen or wiled away from the Church. He planned to restore the fabric of the churches and to reform the morals of the clergy, and he laboured in all ways "to bring the kingdom of Ireland to a conformity in worship, doctrine, and discipline with the Church of England." He procured Laud to be chosen Chancellor of the University of Dublin. A High Commission Court was established, and the same ecclesiastical policy which harassed England and incensed Scotland was pursued in Ireland, not without some success in temporal matters. In the matter of doctrine, however, there still remained much to be accomplished if Wentworth's designs were to be fulfilled.

Wentworth claims Connaught for the Crown.—Pending the conversion of the recusants to the right way, the Deputy busied himself in snatching more lands and money for the King. The victims were the Connaught landowners, whose titles had been purposely left unconfirmed. The Deputy claimed the whole province for the Crown, in right of the ancient Conquest of Henry II., and on similar remote pleas. Roscommon, Sligo, and Mayo at once submitted; but in Galway the jury dared to dispute the King's right, saying that Henry II.'s only title was the willing submission of the inhabitants. In anger the Deputy brought the refractory jury to trial. They were fined four thousand pounds each, and sentenced to imprisonment till it was paid; they were further required to make acknowledgment, upon their knees in court and at the assizes, of their offence in refusing to base their verdict upon the evidence produced. This sentence was duly passed and recorded, though it was never completely executed. Juries in future were not emboldened to oppose the wish of the Deputy, and the King's title to Connaught was accordingly acknowledged. Money, however, was more useful than land; so in most cases the landowners were not dispossessed, but allowed to retain possession on payment of heavy fines. In this respect only Wentworth was impartial in his treatment of the two nationalities. English gold was every whit as good as Irish, and the City of London, having failed to fulfil some of the covenants whereby

F

it held Coleraine, was brought to book, and the Star Chamber fined it £70,000. Thus in many ways Wentworth gathered in money for the King, and for the support of the Irish army which was intended to crush the liberties of England.

Wentworth encourages Irish Trade. — One good thing Wentworth did in Ireland—he strove earnestly to encourage Irish trade, and to remove the burdens imposed on it. He allowed no new monopolies to be granted; he cleared the Irish Sea of pirates, so that the merchandize of Ireland might be safely conveyed away. It is true he discouraged the Irish woollen manufacture lest it should injure the wool trade of England; but to recompense the people for this he brought flax seed and skilled workmen from the Continent, and greatly improved the linen manufacture, which still flourishes in Ireland.

Fall of Strafford, 1640.—In 1640 Wentworth was created Earl of Strafford and Lord-Lieutenant of Ireland; but troubles in England soon put an end to his rule. The King in his hopeless struggle to impose an absolute rule on the people of England and Scotland called to his trusty servant for help. Money and men were forthcoming from well-dragooned Ireland; but both were wasted by Charles I. The anger of the people of England, not yet daring openly to attack the monarch, fell upon his agent, Strafford. He was impeached in England, and condemned to death: he died for his sins against the liberties of England, not of Ireland. That unhappy country, seething with rage and grievances new and old drifted on to the insurrection of 1641.

CHAPTER IV.

THE CROMWELLIAN SETTLEMENT.

The Outbreak of the Rebellion, 1641.—The great rebellion of 1641, sudden as its outburst might seem to the superficial observer, had in reality been long preparing. Persecution and spoliation had kindled anger and hatred against the English, and had inspired, not without reason, a universal dread of further oppression. Events in England and Scotland hastened and encouraged the Irish to revolt. A rumour spread that the Scots were coming over—Bible in one hand, sword in the other—to root out Roman Catholicism, and the rumour intensified the growing fear and thirst for vengeance.

The flame burst out in Ulster. An attempt was made to seize Dublin Castle, but it failed through the treachery of one of the conspirators, and the Pale remained for a while unaffected by the rebellion which raged in the North. Lord Chichester writes to the King: "The Irish, in the northern parts of your Majesty's kingdom of Ireland, two nights last past, did rise with force, and have taken Charlimont, Dongannon, Tonragee, and the Newry, with your Majesty's stores there—townes all of good consequence, the farthest within forty miles of this place, and have slain only one man, and they are advancing near to these parts."

Extract from the Official Report of the Rebellion.—Steadily and swiftly the Ulster men advanced in their work of uprooting and driving out. Every English man, woman, and child was ruthlessly torn from home and driven away, towards Dublin and the English Pale. The contemporary "Report" says: "The city of Dublin is the common receptacle of these miserable sufferers. Here are many thousands of poor people, sometimes of good respects and estates, now in want and sickness, whereof many daily die, notwithstanding the great care of those tender-hearted Christians (whom God bless); without whom all of them had before now perished. . . . We, with such other of our brethren, ours and their wives and children, coming on foot hither through ways tedious and full of peril, being every minute assaulted, the end of one but leading to the next danger, one quite stripping off what others had in pity left. So that in nakedness we have recovered this our city of refuge, where we live in all extremity of want, not having wherewithal to subsist, or to put bread in our mouths. Of those of our brethren who have perished on the way hither, some of their wives and children do yet remain. The children also of some of them are wholly deprived of their parents and left for deserted orphans."

Conduct of the Lords Justices.—The strange conduct of the Lords Justices, in delaying to deal with the rebellion, and their obstinate determination, when at length they were roused to action, to push the Irish to desperation by their hard and unconciliatory attitude and measures, can only be accounted for by accepting the truth of the common rumour—that they thirsted for new lands in confiscation, and so allowed, and even caused, the spread of the rebellion. The opponents of the King in England aided the Lords Justices in this matter.

Act of 1641 *and its consequences.*—The Act passed in December, 1641, which doomed the Roman Catholic religion in Ireland to extinction, changed the face of affairs. The rebellion of Ulster became the rebellion of all Ireland. Anglo-Norman and Celt, moderate and loyal Catholics, as well as obstinate and rebellious recusants, men of all shades of political opinion, joined the ranks of the rebels : the long war of race suddenly became a more deadly war—a war of religion. It was the Catholic against the Protestant, against the stern and unyielding Puritan.

General view of the Rebellion.—It is impossible in this brief sketch to unravel the twisted threads of the history of this great rebellion. Charles I. meddled with it in his dark and tortuous way, and it was not always clear that the rebels were not fighting under the King's orders. In England the power was steadily leaving the King and going to the Parliament, and it is certain that it was no new idea with Charles to fight against his rebels in England with a faithful Irish army. English affairs were too urgent to allow the Long Parliament to engage seriously in the work of suppressing the rebellion. In the early spring of 1642 however they invited the English nation at large to provide money for the purpose, offering portions of the fair and coveted land of Ireland to all who would come forward. This act increased the frenzy of the Irish people, who saw that they themselves were to disappear with their religion. They pressed on to the fray in blind rage, quickened by terror, and the soldiers charged with the duty of opposing them caught the fury, and acted with the utmost cruelty, so that this rebellion and its suppression are marked by terrible scenes of horror. There were many murders on both sides, and many deaths from exposure and hard usage; but the fable, invented and circulated by the enemies of the Irish nation and the coveters of the Irish land, that the rebellion began with a wholesale and organized massacre, is proved, by an accumulation of weighty testimony, to be absolutely untrue.

For more than seven years Ireland was distracted by endless faction and intrigue. The general situation is thus described by a recent writer: "While the wavering struggle between the King and the Parliament was going on in England, four factions, like four vipers twining together in inextricable confusion, fought, conspired, and intrigued in Ireland—the Catholic confederates, the Catholic nobility of the Pale, the Protestant Royalists, and the Parliamentarians." Last of all came the "curse o' Crummell," as it was generally, and not unjustly, called.

Cromwell Lands in Ireland, 1649.—On the 14th of August, 1649, Cromwell landed in Ireland. At his coming all disorderly warfare ceased: his stern and terrible soldiers, carrying out as they believed a divine mission, proceeded to the work of conquest, which in their hands proved to be little less than extermination. Stronghold fell after stronghold, massacre succeeded massacre. That of Drogheda was the worst. Cromwell stayed less than a year in Ireland, but he broke the back of the Irish resistance. Fire, the sword, and starvation are potent weapons. Cromwell and his successors in command so wielded them, that when peace was made, in 1652, Ireland lay exhausted and helpless. Over 600,000 men, women, and children, being one-third of the entire population, had perished. Corn and cattle had been destroyed, the land lay waste, and was ravaged by wolves.

The Settlement Planned.—The time had come for a fresh plantation, to be effected on a larger scale than had ever been attempted before ; but fire, the sword, hunger and pestilence, had not even yet sufficiently cleared the land. Foreign princes were allowed to recruit in Ireland, and over 30,000 of the flower of the Irish nation sailed away to join the armies of Spain, France, and Poland. Many thousands of women and children were sold into West Indian slavery. The wasted people hardly dared to cry out against their doom. They were to be driven bodily out of the three provinces of Ulster, Munster, and Leinster, and penned up in barren Connaught, which was a convenient land for the purposes of banishment and isolation, being almost an island, surrounded by the sea and the Shannon. Then the three emptied provinces were to be planted with English settlers. Land to the value of £360,000 was due to the adventurers who had advanced money ten years before for the army of Ireland. These adventurers were to draw lots for their land. The Government kept for its own purposes four counties—Dublin, Kildare, Carlow, and Cork; also all towns and all Church lands. The rest of Ireland was to be for the officers and soldiers of the army, about to be disbanded.

The Irish Ordered to Transplant, 1653.—In the

year 1653, on the 26th of September, Ireland was declared to be the property of the English soldiers and adventurers, and the Irish were ordered to transplant themselves to Connaught. On every man, woman, or child, of Irish race left east of the Shannon after May 1st, 1654, was pronounced sentence of death. A mockery of an exception was made. Those Irish who could prove that they had borne a constant good affection to the Parliament of England were allowed to stay; but to prove that constant good affection was almost beyond the power of man. A cry, a despairing cry, for time rose up from the afflicted nation. Might they be suffered to gather in their last harvest? Grudgingly this leave was given. Connaught was so bleak and bare that the unhappy ones tried hard to avoid the journey. But the hirelings of the Government and the English thirsting for land kept a stern guard, and hounded them out. Prison and death were to some preferable to transplanting. In the year 1655, on April 3rd, one Edward Hetherington was hanged; and on his back and his breast were displayed the words, "For not transplanting." A letter written from Dublin in the same year says: "The business of transplanting is not yet finished. The Irish in many places choose death rather than remove from their wonted habitations. But the State is resolved to see it done."

The State resolved, but resolutions are not always carried out. To drive out the Irish from their homes, to lay waste the land, and plant it with English, that was accomplished; but to keep those English from the subtle Irish spell was not possible. The plan was—leaving Connaught as an Irish state, and the

THE CROMWELLIAN SETTLEMENT. 73

Pale as an English state—to plant the rest of Ireland with settlers who should keep as labourers certain Irish authorized to remain. These Irish were to be Anglicized. They were to speak the English language, to copy the English manners, to conform to the English Protestant worship, to leave their Irish names, especially the Os and the Macs, and to build chimneys like the English. These strict ordinances, like many others of like import, failed greatly of their purpose. The towns of Ireland seized upon by the English Parliament were emptied of their inhabitants, and in some cases planted with English settlers. Sometimes the English settlers were not forthcoming, then the towns fell into ruins.

The Desolation of Ireland.—The Cromwellian settlement left Ireland desolate. Five-sixths of the population had perished or gone over seas. The wretched ones who remained were preyed upon by wolves. Those in whom any spirit was left fled out into the wilds and became Tories, as they were called. The desolate land was ravaged by three great plagues, said Major Morgan, member for Wicklow County in 1657. " We have three beasts to destroy that lay burthens upon us. The first is the wolf . . . the second beast is a priest . . . the third beast is a Tory." In hunting these beasts the loyal settlers spent their time. The second beast gave terrible trouble; for although the Roman Catholic religion was strictly prohibited by law it still grew and flourished, and persecution only strengthened its power. The dispossessed and exasperated Irish fled beyond the reach of the law, and formed secret and murderous bands which became an abiding terror to the planters. Gentlemen were treacherously called by familiar voices from their fireside, and basely murdered on their own thresholds; others were shot dead as they walked unsuspiciously about their grounds and lands, and the murderers escaped undetected. All attempts to bring the criminals to justice were frustrated by the inability of the English to speak the Irish language, and by the sympathy of Irish with Irish, which induced the innocent to screen the guilty.

CHAPTER V.

THE WARS OF WILLIAM III.

The Restoration, 1660.—The accession of Charles II. raised hopes in the minds of the dispossessed Irish. They prayed the new King to re-establish them in their lands; but he did not dare to disturb to any serious extent the recent settlements. He ousted some few of the English, and restored a few of the Irish; but the general balance of wealth and power remained as left by the Cromwellian settlement. Outward quiet and comparative prosperity marked the reign of Charles II. in Ireland. In the brief reign of his brother and successor hope again stirred in the Irish breast. The Irish Catholics raised their heads, and rivalled James II. in his insolence and folly.

In the turmoil of the Revolution and the years that followed it Ireland became the battle-ground of the long strife which then disturbed Europe—the strife in which despotism, civil and religious, was personated by Louis XIV. of France, and freedom found a champion in William III. of England. Louis saw that if James II. could become the Catholic King of Catholic Ireland, and thence reconquer England, and rule as the willing and grateful slave of France, William would be worsted, and practically Protestantism and freedom throughout

Europe would have received a blow from which it would not easily recover. Therefore help from France was freely given to James.

An army was not indeed given by Louis XIV.; for an army under Tyrconnel only awaited the landing of James in Ireland; but all else necessary for a campaign was forthcoming—arms, money, generals, and last, but not least, a French diplomatist, who should guide all things in the interests of France—the Count of Avaux.

James II. lands in Ireland, 1689.—Parties were sharply divided and warfare already afoot when, early in 1689, James II. landed in Ireland. The leading spirit in the land was Richard Talbot, Earl of Tyrconnel, who, first as Commander-in-chief of the forces in Ireland, then as Lord-Deputy, had laboured assiduously, and with great success, to convert the Protestant ascendancy in that land into Catholic ascendancy. From all important posts, civil and military, from the rank and file of the army, and from the Parliament, Protestants had disappeared, and Catholics had taken their place. Many leading Protestants had fled to England; those who remained were crushed and dumb, except in the two towns of Enniskillen and Londonderry. The Catholics met James II. with much enthusiasm and loyalty. They looked to him to establish them in their religion and in the lands which they had lost under the Cromwellian settlement, and for that reward they were ready to fight for him to the death. Here was the difficulty of James II.'s position. To content the Irish Catholics would be to discontent the English and Scotch Protestants, and so to shut himself off for ever from his lost Kingdoms. This was by no means his wish. He therefore set himself to the task, impossible in that age, of winning all Ireland by conciliating Catholics and Protestants alike. James II. landed at Kinsale on March 12th, 1689. He made his way to Dublin, conciliating and befriending the Protestants as he went. He summoned a Parliament to meet on the 7th of May, and then betook himself to the North.

James II. goes to the North, 1689.—Enniskillen and Londonderry were the only two strongholds of Protestantism left in Ireland, and against them the armies faithful to James were vainly striving. James joined the besiegers of Londonderry, who were under the command of General Richard Hamilton. The arrival of the King outside the walls of Londonderry only stimulated the energy and devotion of its heroic inhabitants. Lundy, the governor of the city, inclining to surrender and stooping to treachery, roused the fierce anger of the citizens against himself, and was forced to fly. One Major Baker, and a clergyman named Walker, took joint command of the garrison, and encouraged it to a sturdy resistance, in spite of hunger and exhaustion. Word was sent to James II. that any messenger he sent should be fired at, and the baffled King turned southward, leaving with the besiegers two of his foreign allies, Marshal Maumont and General Rosen. In the end the citizens were victorious, and to the men of Londonderry, as well as to the Enniskilleners, belongs the honour of having upheld the cause of Protestantism in Ireland while William of Orange was busy establishing himself on the throne of England.

The Irish Parliament assembles, May, 1689.—James II., after his short and useless visit to the North, returned to Dublin to begin the work of legislation. The Parliament which assembled was almost wholly composed of Catholics, the sons of the men whom Charles II. at his restoration had not dared to reinstate. They went their own way, and James II., to his dismay, found that the Irish Commons were as stubborn as the English. The first act of this Parliament was to acknowledge James II. as King; then money was granted for the King's war, but on one condition only— the reversal of the Cromwellian settlement.

Act of Attainder, 1689.—Side by side with this agrarian measure came the great Act of Attainder, providing that over two thousand of the chief men in Ireland would be declared to be guilty of high treason, and their lands forfeited, if they did not within a short time submit themselves to King James II. It was not really expected that these rebels would return to their allegiance; indeed the King had already in his mind disposed of their lands. He meant to give them to such of his loyal subjects as should be left homeless by the reversal of the Cromwellian settlement. After a session of somewhat more than two months the Parliament was prorogued, towards the end of July, 1689.

Landing of Schomberg, 1689. — A month later General Schomberg arrived, with a small force of about six thousand men, to reduce Ireland to the obedience of William and Mary, already the established sovereigns of England and Scotland. He landed at Carrickfergus, in Ulster, that province which, through the victories of the Enniskilleners and the men of Londonderry, might be considered as already won for William. The rest of Ireland, stirred by native enthusiasm and religious zeal, rose up at his coming, and armed men in great numbers flocked to the standard of James II., who encamped near to Schomberg. The great army of the King, 30,000 in number, was eager to give battle, but the foreign generals, skilled in war, and having no confidence in raw and undisciplined troops, restrained them. The veteran Schomberg, wisely heeding his small numbers and his ignorance of the country, also remained quiet. The two armies sat watching each other through the deluge of an Irish autumn; bad and insufficient food and exposure to the weather brought pestilence to the invaders, and when in November both armies prepared to go into winter quarters, one-third of Schomberg's small force had perished.

The winter of 1689-90 was wasted by James II. in Dublin, while his rival was preparing in England a large force, well armed and provisioned, with which to subdue Ireland. Louis XIV. did his best for his incompetent ally: in return for four Irish regiments drafted into the French service he sent over a force of over 6000 men, trained soldiers, well officered and armed, under the command of Count Lauzun. General Rosen was recalled, and Avaux, who could not get on with the indolent Stuart, returned to France in his company. Lauzun saw at once the danger of James II.'s want of energy; he drew up a paper in which he urged wise and brisk measures of preparation for the field. The King read the paper, agreed in great measure to its suggestions, but still very little was done.

In May, 1690, Schomberg was afoot. His troops, greatly reinforced from England, numbered 30,000 men, well armed and provisioned. He opened the campaign by taking Charlemont, the last strong place faithful to James II. in Ulster. It took James a month to get himself ready for the field. Towards the end of June he betook himself and his army to Dundalk, which he selected for his headquarters.

William III. lands in Ireland, June 14th, 1690.—On the 24th of June, James II. learned that his son-in-law had landed at Carrickfergus ten days before, and was already marching southwards. The position which the Irish army had taken up was not suitable for a battle. Lauzun therefore advised and conducted a retreat towards the valley of the Boyne. The army now led by William III. had gained about 6000 men since, under Schomberg, it opened the campaign. Many nationalities were represented by its soldiers. There were the English, the Englishry of Ireland, the Huguenots of France, Scots, Dutch, Germans, and Danes. These last caused the superstitious Irish to quake with fear; for an old prophecy had said that the descendants of the Ostmen would one day destroy the people of Ireland. William commanded in person; under him among others were the veteran Marshal Schomberg, and his son Count Meinhard Schomberg.

Battle of the Boyne, July 1st, 1690.—William III. was most anxious to press on an engagement; James II. was as anxious to avoid it. The Irish pressed on towards Dublin; the English followed them, and overtook them in the valley of the Boyne. In accordance with his fate James was in an almost desperate position; but there was no help for it now, and the battle must be fought. At daybreak on the following day, July 1st, all were astir. The army of William III. forced the fords of the river, and what followed was rather a rout than a battle. The Irish horse fought bravely,

THE WARS OF WILLIAM.

but in vain; the Irish foot were base in their cowardice. The disciplined French troops under Lauzun were led by him early in the day to a point some miles away from the scene of the chief encounter, in order to secure the line of retreat to Dublin. Thus they were withdrawn from the fight itself, though they did good service in covering the retreat of the Irish. James II., tenderly careful of his safety, did not wait to see the battle out. He made for Dublin, stopped long enough in the capital to sneer at the troops who had lost the day for him, then fled to France to his faithful ally, Louis XIV. His two generals, Lauzun and Tyrconnel, led away the remnant of their army from the field of battle. There was no serious pursuit. Passing through Dublin, they made their way to Limerick, carrying with them the artillery. The victorious army marched to Dublin. A public thanksgiving was held in the Cathedral of St. Patrick, William appearing in state with his crown on his head. The brave old Schomberg, who had perished in the battle, was buried in the cathedral.

Fighting in the West.—From the capital William III. proceeded to take Wexford, Waterford, and other places. Then he made for the West, intending to capture Limerick, and so make an end of the war. Before he reached his destination the face of affairs changed. Lauzun and Tyrconnel declared that Limerick was untenable. They withdrew to Galway, taking with them the foreign troops. The Irish army, 20,000 in number, remained to defend Limerick under the command of Boisselot, a French brigadier. In spite of the gloomy forebodings of Lauzun and his party, the garrison was not unsuccessful in repelling William III. The King had moved in advance of his artillery, and the Irish determined to prevent his recovering it. Under the command of Colonel Patrick Sarsfield an Irish force stole out of Limerick by night, surprised the King's artillery, and destroyed it. Nothing could make up for the loss of the siege-train. After an unsuccessful assault William raised the siege and returned to England, dreading the autumn rains for his soldiers. An expedition under the Earl of Marlborough, which captured Cork and Kinsale, wound up the autumn campaign.

Athlone is taken, 1691.—The year 1691 saw the end of the Irish campaign. The English forces were commanded by Baron Ginkel. In the Irish camp the French general Saint Ruth, somewhat hampered by Tyrconnel, held the chief command. The summer had come before operations began. In June Ginkel attacked the town of Athlone, well fortified, strongly garrisoned, and supported by Saint Ruth, who lay encamped at a short distance. For ten days the besiegers held out; then the town was stormed and taken, chiefly owing to the negligence of Saint Ruth.

The Battle of Aughrim, 1691.—Mortified by this defeat, the French general sought his revenge in a pitched battle. He drew up his forces on the heights of Aughrim, and sought to bar the westward march of the conquerors. Tyrconnel had retired to Limerick. On the 12th of July the English army joined battle, and a terrible fray ensued. The fortune of war long wavered. At length a cannon ball struck down Saint Ruth, and with him passed away the fortunes of the Irish army. Seven thousand fell on the field. The rest fled to Galway and Limerick, the last strongholds of their race.

THE WARS OF WILLIAM. 83

Surrender of Galway and Limerick.—Galway did not long hold out. Ginkel offered a general amnesty and toleration to the Catholics, and the town submitted, wearied with the hopeless struggle; the garrison, with D'Usson, the French commander, retiring to Limerick. All the hope of the Irish was now shut up in Limerick, but that town was as a house divided against itself. D'Usson, Saint Ruth's subordinate and successor, was in favour of stout resistance, hoping to drag on the siege till the autumn rains should drive Ginkel into winter quarters, and counting on fresh help from France in the spring. Tyrconnel, who represented the Irish party, had lost all hope of success; he was only awaiting James II.'s leave to surrender when he died, struck by apoplexy. The brave Sarsfield was then left as head of the Irish party, and the counsel of despair prevailed.

Treaty of Limerick, 1691.—The besieged opened negotiations, and in the name of the Irish people demanded, as a condition of their surrender, freedom for Catholics in the exercise of their religion, and equal civil rights. Though Ginkel did not dare to grant so comprehensive a demand, he went as far as he could. The Treaty of Limerick, as finally concluded, ignored the matter of civil rights, but promised to the Irish Roman Catholics such freedom in their religion as they had enjoyed in the time of King Charles II. The later history of Ireland is a justification of the title that Limerick has since acquired, of "the City of the Broken Treaty." A military treaty gave permission to all Irish soldiers who wished to cling to their ancient cause to enter the French army, and in pursuance of this agreement 12,000 men quitted Ireland for France.

CHAPTER VI.

THE PENAL LAWS.

General View of Irish Affairs in the Eighteenth Century.—The defeated and depopulated country was now to undergo a period of steady oppression, directed, on the one hand, against the religion of the majority; on the other, against the commerce and material prosperity of all. This oppression increased with the years of the eighteenth century. The stir of the Scottish rebellions of 1715 and 1745 found no response in Ireland; but in the minds of the Irish, the thought grew and strengthened, that all their evils came from dependence on England. The successful revolt of the American colonies, and the mutinous temper engendered by it, encouraged the uprising which led to the emancipation of the Irish Parliament in 1782 with all its consequences. It is true that not all the guilt of Irish misery and oppression must be laid on English shoulders. It must be borne in mind that often, when the English government was prepared with wise and liberal measures, the Irish Protestants, narrow and dogmatic, prevented the proper reform. By a sad mischance the good intentions both of English and Irish were seldom carried out.

We must now attempt to chronicle this course of legislation which we have characterized as oppression, beginning with the laws against the Catholics, commonly known as the Penal Code.

The Penal Laws, 1696.—An Act of the English Parliament, passed in 1696, was the first step. It required from members of both Houses of the Irish Parliament the Oaths of Allegiance and Abjuration, and a Declaration against Transubstantiation. Thus the Catholics were virtually expelled. The same requisition was imposed upon "every person holding office ecclesiastical, civil, or military;" so that by a single stroke the Irish Catholics were thrust out of all positions of importance. Then the Irish Parliament, ultra-Protestant in its new form, went on with the work.

An Act was passed forbidding Catholics to send their children abroad for education, or to have them taught at home in any but Protestant schools.

Another Act was passed forbidding Catholics to carry, or even to possess, arms, on penalty, for the first offence, of a heavy fine; for the second, of imprisonment for life and forfeiture of all goods.

In 1698 it was enacted that "all bishops, Jesuits, monks, friars, and 'regular clergy,' should leave Ireland, never to return, on penalty of being hung, drawn, and quartered." The parish priests were allowed to remain; but they were compelled, by an Act passed six years later, to be registered, and to give security for good behaviour.

In 1698 an Act was also passed to prevent the intermarriage of Catholics and Protestants, except in certain specified cases, and to facilitate in those cases the passing of Catholic dowers into Protestant hands.

In 1699 an Act was passed forbidding Catholics to

practise as solicitors without taking the oaths on penalty of £100. This fine was afterwards doubled.

These stringent Acts greatly failed of their purpose. It was always the way in Ireland that savage laws should exist side by side with a weak executive. More laws and stronger were accordingly passed with the intent to take the land from the Catholics, and keep it from them for ever.

In 1704 it was enacted that any one perverting a Protestant should be liable to the penalties of *præmunire;* that is, imprisonment for life, and forfeiture of all goods. Catholics were forbidden to act as guardians under penalty of £500 fine. Catholic fathers were compelled to hand over their Protestant children to guardians of the reformed faith. The eldest son of a Catholic, being a Protestant, inherited all his father's estate; but the Catholic sons of a Catholic father divided the estate, and took share and share alike.

No Catholic was allowed to purchase land or to hold a mortgage on land. A Catholic might not hold a lease of longer than thirty-one years, and that only on certain conditions. After a certain specified date no Catholic might inherit any estate without first changing his faith.

No Catholic might vote at an election without taking the oaths.

No Catholic might settle in Galway or Limerick. Catholics already inhabiting those cities must give security for good behaviour.

All pilgrimages were declared riotous and unlawful. Pilgrims to holy places were ordered to be fined 10s., or whipped at the cart's tail.

In 1710 new and stronger laws were again passed, all with the intent to keep land and learning away from the Catholics, and to encourage informers.

Finally, in 1733, all Catholics were disfranchised, both as regards Parliamentary and municipal elections.

Effect of the Penal Laws.—These laws succeeded in thrusting out of Ireland the flower of the Catholic gentry, who lived and rose to eminence in foreign lands. But they failed to turn from their religion the mass of the peasants, who clung to the land, and grew more and more devoted to their Church.

Commercial Legislation.—In like manner as the Catholics were hunted out of Ireland by the laws against their religion, so were the Protestant colonists reduced to poverty, and finally driven out, by the laws destroying the trade of Ireland.

The commercial legislation was inspired by the fear and jealousy of the English traders. The reign of Charles II. began in Ireland with comparative prosperity. The rich pasture lands brought much trade to the colonists; but lest English farmers should suffer, it was enacted that no Irish cattle nor dairy produce should be imported into England. A great and flourishing trade was thus abolished.

In pursuance of the same policy Ireland was shut off from all trade with the colonies. The Irish wool was esteemed to be the best in Europe: it was feared that it would drive the English wool from the market, and by repeated restrictive Acts the trade in Irish wool was ruined.

In 1699 it was enacted that no Irish manufactured wool should be exported to any country whatever. The flourishing and legitimate trade thus destroyed was replaced by a smuggling trade with France and other Catholic countries.

Thousands of loyal Protestant colonists were driven from Ireland by the restrictions placed on them wherever they turned. The only trade allowed to Ireland was the linen manufacture. It had existed in Ireland from very early times. Strafford, as we have seen, gave it a great impetus; but the restrictions placed on Irish trade prevented it from becoming the source of wealth which it otherwise might have been. It chiefly flourished in the North. To the inhabitants of Leinster, Munster, and Connaught there remained no possible means of gaining a livelihood but that of wresting it from the land, and the whole intent of legislation was to take even the land from the Catholics, who formed the overwhelming mass of the people.

Of the miserable eighteenth century in Ireland the chief facts to be borne in mind are: first, that all the best of the people, old Catholic Irish and new Protestant English, were driven away in despair by the laws which made it penal to exercise the Catholic religion, and to engage in almost any business; secondly, that those who remained clung with desperate devotion to the Church of Rome, and lived in constant opposition to and evasion of the law. They were perpetually being reminded that dependence on the English Parliament was the source of all their ills, and they longed for an opportunity to shake off the yoke. The Act known as the sixth of George I. finally completed their subjection by expressly declaring that "the English Parliament had, hath, and of right ought to have power and authority to make laws and statutes of sufficient force and validity to bind the people and kingdom of Ireland."

THE PENAL LAWS.

Let us briefly chronicle the most salient events of this wretched period from the beginning of the century to the year of the first free Parliament.

Material Misery.—The material misery of the country during the first half of the century, due to many causes, but chiefly to the destruction of trade, bad harvests, and severe winters, can scarcely be exaggerated. The people died by thousands of cold, famine, and fever. Although there are some noble exceptions, the majority of the ruling classes of Ireland from the Viceroy downwards were absentees. For forty years the land was virtually ruled by the Primates—Boulter, Hoadly, and Stone. The business of Parliament, which sat every other year, was in great measure carried on by the bishops. To the doubtful good service of providing rulers of the State the Church added the terrible oppression of the tithes. The wretched peasants, barely able to get from the land food enough for themselves, were yet obliged to give a tenth of all for the support of the alien clergy. Most unfairly, pasture land held by the large graziers did not pay tithes, while the small potato patch was ruthlessly mulcted by the tithe procter. To the hatred of the tithe are attributable the Whiteboy risings of the end of the eighteenth century, and innumerable outrages in the nineteenth. In 1838 this grievance came to an end, when after a long Parliamentary struggle the Act for the Commutation of Tithes was passed.

Dean Swift.—One Churchman indeed did good service to Ireland—Jonathan Swift, Dean of St. Patrick's, the patriot who wielded the most formidable pen of his time. He went to Ireland as Dean of St. Patrick's in 1713, and for many years took an active part in Irish politics, chiefly through his anonymous writings. The most famous of his political pamphlets were *The Drapier's Letters*, which succeeded in defeating an infamous job set on foot by Sir Robert Walpole and the Duchess of Kendal, a German favourite of George I.

Wood's Halfpence, 1723.—It was an old grievance that Ireland possessed no mint, and that private persons coined her money, with more regard for their own gain than for the good of the realm. In 1722, there being a lack of copper coin, save of the most debased kind, the privilege of coining £108,000 of halfpence and farthings was granted to the Duchess of Kendal. The Duchess transferred the patent to a certain Mr. Wood, who began the work of coinage. Over these halfpence arose the greatest storm that had shaken Ireland for many years. The coins were not more debased than Irish money generally was. But they were represented as being the most base of all coins, and Swift declared that thirty-six of them would only suffice to buy a quart of twopenny ale. But the number and badness of the halfpence were really only a small part of the objection to them. The manner of issuing the patent was the gravest infringement of the rights of the Irish nation. It was granted by the English Government to a private person, the Lord-Lieutenant of Ireland, the Privy Council and the Lords and Commons of that realm, being ignored. It was therefore a grievance to be resented by all Irishmen. A storm of protest raged through the land. The Parliament was loud in opposition, the Corporations of the towns spoke out, pamphlets were written, sermons preached, and ballads sung against the halfpence. *The Drapier's Letters*, purporting to come from a Dublin tradesman, were really from the pen of Swift. They began by damning the halfpence, but went on to strike at the dependency of the Irish Parliament, preaching many a sermon from the text, " Government without the consent of the governed is the very definition of slavery," and the Government quaked at the effect of the bold words on the people. The Lord-Lieutenant, the Duke of Grafton, was recalled, and Carteret, afterwards Lord Granville, replaced him; but the new Lord-Lieutenant was as powerless as his predecessor. The English Government was forced to withdraw the patent, and there was an end of the business.

Lord Chesterfield, Lord Harrington, and the Primates.—A political calm of some years followed this violent storm; but the material condition of Ireland underwent no improvement, and agrarian misery was as rife as ever. Nevertheless the troublous times of the '45 glided away without the shadow of a storm under the wise rule of the brilliant Lord Chesterfield. After his short tenure of office came that of Lord Harrington, in whose time Archbishop Stone, the powerful though unpopular successor of Archbishop Boulter, exercised the chief power in the State. In Harrington's time Irish trade again began to hold up its head, and with a surplus came a dispute, protracted and often renewed, as to the right to dispose of it between the Irish Parliament and the King. Parliamentary opposition to English tyranny was strengthened by outside agitation. One Charles Lucas, a Dublin citizen, laboured for the good of his country by his political writings, which had great influence. His great theme was the sole right of the Irish Parliament to legislate for Ireland, and among the reforms which he rightly deemed necessary for his native Parliament was the limiting of its duration. That the raising of this question was not unnecessary may be proved by the fact that the Parliament summoned at the accession of George II. lasted for the thirty-three years of his reign. Lucas aroused the wrath of the Government by his writings, and was exiled in 1749.

Rise of the Patriots.—In the latter half of the century a party arose and strengthened itself in Parliament, whose aim was to govern Ireland through her native Parliament, and to put a stop to the monstrous system of jobbery and corruption of which the affair of Wood and his halfpence was only one example. To avoid disputes as to the right of dealing with a surplus the Opposition laboured to prevent the accumulation of a surplus, and great sums of public money were spent on public works. Repeated efforts were made to cut down the pension list, a continual scandal, but in vain. That there should have been any honest party in the Parliament was a marvel. The great majority of the seats were in the hands of a few powerful men—the "Undertakers," who undertook to lead affairs in the English interest, and in return were masters of most of the patronage of the Crown.

During the Seven Years' War the trade of Ireland suffered to a great extent. The potato failed, and there was terrible misery in the land. "The bulk of the people," writes Primate Stone, in 1758, "are not regularly either lodged, clothed, or fed."

The tendency of the time was to turn arable land into pasture, especially when a plague among English and Continental cattle, by raising the price of the beasts, gave the Irish a chance of making some money. This change threw great numbers of poor people out of employment. Besides this, those who were left on the soil suffered a great wrong by the inclosure of common lands. This matter of the inclosures, together with the old grievance of the tithes, brought into existence a widespread and powerful secret organization, the first of all the secret societies, which have from that time gnawed at the heart of Ireland. The parents of the Irish Invincibles were the Whiteboys.

The Whiteboys, 1761.—John Wesley tells in his Journal, June, 1762, of their first appearing. "About the beginning of December last a few men met by night near Nenagh, in the county of Limerick, and threw down the fences of some commons which had been lately inclosed. Near the same time others met in the counties of Tipperary, Waterford, and Cork. As no one offered to suppress or hinder them they increased in numbers continually, calling themselves Whiteboys, wearing white cockades and white linen frocks. In February there were five or six parties of them, 200 to 300 men in each, who moved up and down chiefly in the night . . . levelled a few fences, dug up some grounds, and hamstrung some cattle, perhaps fifty or sixty in all. One body of them came into Clogheen, of about 500 foot and 200 horse. They moved as exactly as regular troops, and appeared to be thoroughly disciplined."

The Whiteboys, under the command of "Captain Right," spread throughout the length and breadth of the land, plundering and destroying, by way of redressing the wrongs of the Irish. For five years they harassed the country, and the law was almost powerless. Then stringent Coercion Acts were passed, and by dint of stern and steady repression the Whiteboys were in great measure put down, though for twenty years afterwards there were risings in various localities. The disaffection was not trampled out, but only thrust underground.

The Oakboys, 1762.—In the North a milder outbreak occurred, partly caused by the tithes, partly by a grievance about the making of the roads. The aggrieved Northerners, their heads decked with boughs of oak, went about in warlike fashion, and threatened the clergy and laity until they got their way.

The Steelboys, 1768.—The Steelboys, or Heart o' Steelboys, who arose in 1771, were the ejected peasantry of Ulster, who, stung to desperation by the ruin of themselves and their families, committed deeds of destruction and violence. Stern measures were taken, and the Steelboys vanished, fleeing to America.

The Parliament frets under Poynings' Law.—To return to the constitutional history. The second part of Poynings' law enacted that when Parliament was about to assemble the Irish Privy Council should send to the English Privy Council the heads of the bills about to be brought forward, and custom ruled that one of these bills should be a money bill. This custom of a money bill originating in the Privy Council always angered the Commons and irritated whatever independent feeling existed throughout the country. The accession of George III. was marked by a very strong protest on this subject, within and without the House; but the protest was ineffectual.

Lord Halifax Lord-Lieutenant.—There was great excitement at the general election of 1760, and this is not surprising, since a generation had passed since Ireland had seen a general election. Lord Halifax was George III.'s first Lord-Lieutenant, and under him the Roman Catholics made earnest supplication to be allowed to serve in the King's armies. The judgment of those in power could not agree to admit them into the king's armies in England; but a scheme was set afoot for admitting Irish Roman Catholic regiments into the allied army of Portugal. The scheme came to nothing, but through no fault of the Catholics.

The points of reform on which the patriots were bent were—Immovability of judges, Habeas Corpus Act, restriction of pensions, and limitation of the duration of Parliament. These measures were brought in and suppressed.

The Undertakers are replaced by a Resident Lord-Lieutenant.—Five years after the accession of George III. came a further change in Irish affairs. It was resolved to do away with the Undertakers, and to have a resident Lord-Lieutenant, who should rule in earnest. It was difficult to find any one to pilot the ship through the distressed Irish seas. Three shadows of Viceroys flitted across the scene, then came the stout Lord Townshend, a soldier, with bluff, good-humoured, undignified ways, whose lavish hospitality made him at once popular. His utter ignorance of State affairs led him into a pitfall, however, at the very outset of his rule. He had been instructed to coax men over to the Government side by dangling before them the satisfaction of the popular demands. Not understanding vague and underhand ways, he boldly promised, in the speech from the throne, the immovability of the judges. The English authorities had no intention of granting this reform. They got out of the difficulty by so altering the Bill in England that the Irish Parliament rejected it on its return as not fulfilling their intention. The whole strength of the Irish patriots was turned to trying to pass a Septennial Bill. The whole strength of the English party was turned to trying to augment the army to 15,000 men. A course of bargaining began. The view of the English party was, "More soldiers are wanted for the Empire at large. The English Parliament will not grant them, we will squeeze them out of Ireland." The Irish view was, "Our army is already 12,000 men, more than we want; in fact, we always do with far less, for the most of them are on foreign service. But we want to get something out of you, namely, the Septennial Bill; so we will grant you the augmentation if you grant us our Bill. Also we make this condition: If we support 15,000 men, 12,000 must be always in Ireland, to put down our Whiteboys, Oakboys, and Steelboys; also grant no more pensions and tax absentees."

Octennial Act and Augmentation Act Passed.—In November, 1767, the Bill for shortening the duration of Parliament passed in Ireland. It was an Octennial Bill, to suit the special circumstances of Ireland, where Parliament only sat every other year, and also to avoid the general confusion which, it was supposed, would arise if the English and Irish elections coincided.

Then came the wish of the King's heart—the Augmentation Bill. The Undertakers—Lord Shannon, Ponsonby, and Hely Hutchinson—asked too high a price for their support. The Government could not or would not give it, and the triumvirate went into opposition. Townshend had never counted on their support as permanent; he now cast about how to remove them, and to create a majority subservient to himself. Much underhand work preceded the session of 1769, and a sudden storm marked its opening.

The unpopular Money Bill was sent over as usual from the Irish Privy Council to England, as a cause for summoning the new Parliament. It was returned to Ireland according to custom, and it was rejected by the Irish Parliament, a resolution being passed to the effect that the Bill was rejected "because it did not take its rise in the House of Commons." The English Government, having an immediate point to carry, dissembled. The resolution was received in silence. The Augmentation Bill was carried, and liberal supplies voted for two years. Then Lord Townshend, having got all that he wanted for the present, solemnly protested against the resolution, as being an infringement of Poynings' law, and prorogued Parliament for fourteen months.

The general wrath of the nation was aroused at this prorogation. Famine, distress, and disaffection combined to make the state of things very bad. Meanwhile Townshend followed out his plan of overthrowing the Undertakers, and building up the power of the Lord-Lieutenant. Lord Shannon and Mr. Ponsonby were deprived of office, together with all the lesser men who dared to oppose the Government.

Corruption in every form succeeded in creating a majority for the Lord-Lieutenant, and the Parliament, which opened on February 26th, 1771, was as subservient as could be desired. Mr. Ponsonby resigned the Speakership, and Mr. Pery was elected in his stead.

End of Lord Townshend's Tenure of Office.—The

reign of Lord Townshend, which began with such pleasant promise, dragged itself out to a dismal end in 1772. An infamous job marked its close. Being in need of more offices to bestow, the Lord-Lieutenant bethought himself that he might divide the Boards of Custom and Excise, and make more Commissioners of Account. Public opinion, both in the House and out of it, was strong against this step; but, trusting in his popularity, Lord Townshend persisted, until the cry against him grew loud and bitter. His disreputable and disgraceful private life gave his enemies a great handle against him, and his public life was equally assailable.

Lord Harcourt Lord-Lieutenant, 1772.—At last in very shame Lord Townshend was recalled, and Lord Harcourt, a man of venerable age and tranquil disposition, was sent over in his stead, in 1772. He made friends with the chief men—Shannon, Leinster, Ponsonby, and Flood—but he committed himself to no course of action during the year which passed between his accession to power and the meeting of Parliament. He won for himself golden opinions in his first session by undoing Lord Townshend's excise arrangements.

Lord Harcourt fails to impose a Tax on Absentees.—Finance was in a wretched condition, and it was necessary for the Viceroy to find some means of relieving it. He came to the conclusion that the best remedy was the ancient one of a tax of two shillings in the pound on the rent of absentees. This was very unpopular in England, and excited much discussion in both countries. Lord Chatham was in favour of it, on the ground that it was the wish of the Irish

Commons, who ought to rule over their country's purse. Edmund Burke was against it, and, at the request of the great English Whigs, he penned a remonstrance, which was scattered broadcast. So strong an influence was brought to bear against this tax that it was rejected, and the money so urgently needed was raised by a batch of new duties.

Flood takes Office and loses his Power.—Lord Harcourt made two important appointments when he had finished the Parliament business. He made Hely Hutchinson provost of Trinity College, Dublin, and Henry Flood vice-treasurer. On the matter of Flood's appointment there was much to be said, especially by the patriots; for Flood had been their leader, and they bitterly resented his taking office. Flood always alleged that he took office because he conceived that only so could he do his country any good. But from this time his popular influence waned, and his place was taken by Henry Grattan, the most noble of Irish patriots, and the most brilliant of Irish orators, whose upright and single mind gained him the respect of all. From this time onwards to the Union, and for long after, he is the central figure in Irish politics.

The American Address.—When Grattan first entered Parliament, the longing of Ireland for a free Parliament was stimulated by a voice from America. The same problem was agitating England's subjects on both sides of the sea, and in 1775 the Americans sent an address to the Irish, pointing out that both peoples were in one case, and asking for help; yet so little could the Parliament be depended on for reflecting the will of Ireland, that the Address in reply to the royal speech, at the beginning of the session of 1775, strongly reprehended the conduct of the Americans, and some Irish troops were actually sent over to help to quell the colonists' rebellion.

Lord Harcourt Departs, 1776.—Lord Harcourt departed from Ireland at the end of 1776, leaving behind him a country overwhelmed with misery. The annual expenses of government had enormously increased under the corrupt *régime* of the resident viceroys. Trade, owing partly to the stern English restrictions, was at a very low ebb. It was absolutely necessary that Ireland should provide money, for her own wants and those of her mistress; therefore, reluctantly, a scheme was drawn up for relaxing some of the crushing restrictions which took the life out of Irish trade. From every English merchant, save the men of London, arose a cry of jealous resistance; and concession, which could not be entirely withheld, was pared down to the narrowest limits. But the very smallest of concessions was valuable for the sake of principle and precedent.

Remedial Legislation.—Ireland was at last beginning to shake off the tremendous double yoke which for so many years had weighed upon her. The will of the people was beginning to exercise its strength. Side by side with the trade concessions came concessions to the Catholics. Not from any sense of abstract justice, but from sheer necessity and lack of soldiers, did England allow the recruiting of Irish Catholics. In the meantime the restrictions which kept the Catholics from owning land, or in any way being interested in the holding or cultivation of land, were being gradually thrust aside. The entire loyalty of the Catholics as such during the various disturbances of the century took away all reasonable objection to their enfranchise-

THE PENAL LAWS.

ment. In 1774 an Act was passed to enable Catholics to swear allegiance before a justice of the peace. The Catholics, who had now so long been inert as far as any social or political action was in question, became with each concession, minute though it was, more keen and eager for enfranchisement.

The Catholic Association.—A Catholic Association had been formed in 1759. Its object was to watch over the interests of Catholics in every possible way. The Irish Protestants met their Catholic brethren halfway. Tolerance, and not fanaticism, was the fashion of the day; moreover the patriot, seeking to free his country, could not leave out the greater part of her inhabitants. Grattan's saying, "The Irish Protestant could never be free till the Irish Catholic had ceased to be a slave," was the key to the action of the patriots on this matter of the enfranchisement of the Catholics.

In 1778 the Catholics presented a petition asking for relief, and in the same year a Bill was passed which may be looked upon as the beginning of the downfall of the Penal Code. By this bill Catholics were enabled to hold and inherit land, and the odious system by which children were induced to change their religion in order to despoil their parents was abolished. Lawful agitation sufficed to obtain these first pledges of reform for Irish merchants and Irish Catholics. To gain political freedom Ireland was obliged to have recourse to the sword.

CHAPTER VII.

THE VOLUNTEERS.

The Volunteers, 1778.—The year 1778 saw Ireland in an utterly defenceless state. The enemies of England were watching, it was feared, for an opportunity of striking a blow through her disaffected province, and that province, though she paid for the support of 15,000 of the king's troops, was left with not one-third of the number, a force totally insufficient to protect her. Waiving the question of the misappropriation of the forces meant to defend the country, the gentlemen of Ireland were most anxious that a militia should be formed, or, failing that, that companies of volunteers should be raised. A militia was out of the question; for the Government was penniless. It had come then to this, that Ireland was in imminent danger and her mistress could do nothing for her. With no anger or resentment, but with the noble fervour of pure patriotism, the men of Ireland, gentle and simple, rose up and formed an army of over forty thousand men, loyal to England.

The chief men in Ireland, amongst others the Duke of Leinster and Lord Charlemont, were at the head of the movement. The Lord-Lieutenant looked on with alarm at the rise of this great armed force outside his control, which, loyal and disciplined, and assembled for a lawful and unimpeachable purpose, could not be touched.

General misery.—The volunteers were not the only cause of alarm to Lord Buckingham. Dire distress and disaffection filled the land. The miserable lack of trade reduced thousands to starvation. When the country at large starved the government could not flourish. There was not one penny of money in the treasury, and for means to meet the most pressing and immediate calls the Lord-Lieutenant was indebted to one Mr. La Touche, a Dublin banker, who advanced £20,000. The widespread belief, certainly not without foundation, that the restrictions on trade were the cause of the distress, produced a loud cry for free trade. The stout resistance of the American colonists to the policy of England had a decided influence in Ireland. An address, urging upon the Irish community of interests, came from America, and was sent up and down the land. The cry for practical reform came from the heart of a people longing for political freedom. Concession to Irish trade was to be the thin end of the wedge.

Parliament meets, 1779.—Parliament met in October, 1779, and the first step towards Irish freedom was taken. The address to the Crown urged that "free trade" should be granted; only a short Money Bill was passed. No permanent taxes were to be granted until the grievances were redressed. The words and deeds of the Parliament men were emphasized by the volunteers, and threatening crowds gathered about the streets of the city. "England has sown her lands," said a patriot, "in dragon's teeth, and they have sprung up in armed men."

Fear of the volunteers prevailed, and in 1779 England began to try to do justice to Ireland. Trade with the colonies and with the Levant was thrown open to Ireland. The country was not ungrateful for this concession, but the thought ran through all minds that the hand which gave might take away. The presence of the volunteers emboldened all, and Ireland demanded that her Parliament should be free.

Irish Declaration of Independence, 1780.—On April 19th, 1780, Grattan moved for the first time the Irish Declaration of Independence :

"Resolved,—

"(1) That His most excellent Majesty, by and with the consent of the Lords and Commons of Ireland, are the only power competent to enact laws to bind Ireland.

"(2) That the Crown of Ireland is and ought to be inseparably annexed to the Crown of Great Britain.

"(3) That Great Britain and Ireland are inseparably united under one sovereign, under the common and indissoluble ties of interest, loyalty, and freedom."

The speech accompanying these resolutions was a masterpiece of eloquence, but it failed of its immediate purpose. By corrupt means the Government had secured so great a majority in the House of Commons, that it was not possible to pass the resolutions, and the debate was adjourned indefinitely.

The second Irish assault took the form of a Bill to prevent the Irish Privy Council from altering or suppressing Bills on their way to the King. This Bill was brought in by Yelverton and rejected. The third Irish assault was inspired by the strong feeling that English laws were not binding in Ireland. It was said that there was nothing to keep the army in order, and Gervase Burke brought in an Irish Mutiny Bill. It was passed and sent to England, and there altered in the important point of duration. The clause which made the Bill an annual one was cut out; and so subservient was the majority in the Irish Parliament, that the Bill was actually passed in its altered form; so that the control of the army passed away from Parliament, and the army became a tool in the King's hands. This action filled the people with anger against the majority.

Lord Carlisle Lord-Lieutenant, 1780.—Lord Buckingham, worn out with his thankless task, was now recalled, and Lord Carlisle, a promising young man and a great friend of Charles James Fox, succeeded him, Sir W. Eden, afterwards the first Lord Auckland, being the new Chief Secretary. The new Viceroy found Ireland still in imminent danger of foreign invasion, but light at heart on that score because of her splendid volunteer army. Many successful reviews were held in the summer of 1781. The volunteers, who not long after their first assembling numbered 40,000 men, now counted nearly double that number. They were strong enough to protect their country from foreign invasion, and they determined also to free her from domestic tyranny. The repeal of Poynings' law, that ancient yoke, was the thing longed for; but the session of 1781 did not obtain it. Only a Habeas Corpus Act was extorted from England in this year. There was a general longing to do justice to the Roman Catholics, and a Relief Bill was discussed. All were agreed that there should be liberty of worship and liberty of holding land. But there was naturally a disinclination to upset the land settlement, and so men were divided as to whether political power should be given to the Catholics.

The will of Ireland, manifest in the volunteers, was now determined to march on to freedom. The slow and painful wresting of point after point could no longer be endured.

Convention of Dungannon, 1782.—It was resolved to hold a Convention of the chief volunteers of Ulster, which would practically be a true Parliament. At noon on the 15th of February, 1782, the delegates, 242 in number, met in the Church of Dungannon. They debated for eight hours and passed several resolutions, of which the following are the chief :

" 1. That a claim of any body of men, other than the King, Lords, and Commons of Ireland, to make laws to bind this kingdom is unconstitutional, illegal, and a grievance.

" 2. That the powers exercised by the Privy Council of both kingdoms under, or under colour or pretence of, the law of Poyning, are unconstitutional and a grievance.

" 3. That we hold the right of private judgment, in matters of religion, to be equally sacred in others as in ourselves; that we rejoice in the relaxation of the PENAL LAWS against our ROMAN CATHOLIC FELLOW-SUBJECTS, and that we conceive the measure to be fraught with the happiest consequences to the union and prosperity of the inhabitants of Ireland."

One Colonel Irvine presided at the Convention, and Lord Charlemont, Mr. Flood, Mr. Grattan, Mr. Stewart (the father of Lord Castlereagh), and Francis Dobbs were among the most prominent members. Before they separated they resolved to meet again in a year's time. Committees were appointed to act meanwhile, and, with four exceptions, every member swore to vote for no Parliamentary candidate who did not pledge himself to work for the fulfilment of the resolutions.

The thunder of Dungannon echoed in the Parliament House. For the second time Grattan moved the Irish Declaration of Independence; for the second time the obsequious majority rejected it. But a change was at hand. In the spring of the year 1782-3 Lord North's government came to an end. A Whig ministry under Lord Rockingham took office. The Duke of Portland was sent over as Lord-Lieutenant. Two days after his arrival the Parliament assembled in Dublin. The city was thronged; the volunteers, gathered in thousands, watched the march of events. On the 16th of April, 1782, Grattan moved for the third time the Irish Declaration of Independence. The most splendid eloquence flowed from his lips; in him appeared incarnate "the whole faculty of the nation . . . braced up to the act of her own deliverance." The threefold chain of Poynings' law, the sixth of George I., and the Perpetual Mutiny Act, was now to be struck off.

That England must yield admitted of no doubt; but the Government made an effort to delay, and to concoct a treaty which should define the relations of the two countries. Grattan would listen to no delay, no treaty. Ireland's rights must first be restored, then negotiation might come. He was obeyed.

The Irish Parliament Unshackled, 1782.—The English Parliament repealed the sixth of George I., forbade the Privy Councils of England and Ireland to mutilate or suppress bills, and limited the Mutiny Act to two years.

An address of thanks to the King was moved by Grattan in the Irish House of Commons, large sums for the British navy were voted, over 3000 of the Irish troops were placed at the disposal of England. A solemn day of thanksgiving was held. Acts granting relief to Catholics were also passed, and the first free Irish Parliament showed its grateful love to its liberator by voting a grant of £50,000 to Henry Grattan.

CHAPTER VIII.

THE INDEPENDENT IRISH PARLIAMENT.

Agitation for Parliamentary Reform and Catholic Emancipation, 1783.—The English gift of a free Parliament for Ireland was little better than a specious promise, which ended in bitter disappointment. That a body so constituted as the Irish Parliament, ignoring the great Catholic majority of the nation, and very imperfectly and corruptly representing the Protestant minority, could adequately govern was a thing impossible. Without Parliamentary Reform and Catholic Emancipation legislative independence was of no avail. The English Government would not grant these two points; perhaps they could not have done so without danger to the connection.

The Plan of the Union.—The Union, that great solution of the Irish difficulty, floated always before the eyes of Pitt, who became Prime Minister in 1783; but as usual no definite policy was pursued in Ireland save the policy of corruption. Stoutly to resist the demand for reform, steadily to gather up all power into the hands of the government through the Parliamentary majority, then to drift wheresoever the general tendency of things should lead, those were the views to be adopted by the English executive in Ireland. That the Union was the ultimate end was never doubted and never avowed. How the persistent denial of such reforms as alone could give vitality to the shadowy Irish Parliament so exasperated the people that they broke forth into rebellion, and how that rebellion formed a decent pretext for the Union, must now be told.

Simple Repeal Controversy.—The first important question which stirred the independent Irish Parliament was the question of "Simple Repeal." The Irish Parliament had been placed in subordination to the Parliament of England, according to the English view, by the Act known as Poynings' law; but the force of that law had always been a moot point, the Irish view being that it was not strictly binding. It had, however, been formally confirmed, as we have seen, by the Act passed in 1720, and known as the sixth George I., which expressly declared the subordination of Ireland to the English Parliament; the latter statute was thus clear and indisputable, not ambiguous like the law of Poynings. Hence when the sixth George I. was repealed, the true and consistent Irish view should have been that the Irish Parliament was free; but a difference arose in the Irish ranks. For various reasons, public and personal, Flood and Grattan differed. Grattan held that the Simple Repeal of the sixth of George I. gave Ireland her freedom; Flood held that more was needed. Flood's views prevailed, and in 1783 the Parliament of Great Britain passed a solemn Act of Renunciation, whereby all attempt to control the Irish Parliament by Acts passed only in the English was given up.

On one other important point did Flood and Grattan differ. Both were intensely anxious for Parliamentary reform; but Flood would have forced on reform by means of the power of the volunteers, whereas Grattan held that to be under a military despotism was in itself too great an evil to be borne.

Volunteer Reform Bill.—The Volunteer Convention sat in state in Dublin, and tried to overawe the Parliament. A Reform Bill, comprehensive enough save in the very important point of Catholic Emancipation, was drawn up by the Convention, and this bill Flood introduced into the House of Commons. It was rejected, not on its merits, but because it came from without. The Convention being defeated peaceably dispersed.

All Efforts for Reform frustrated.—That a Reform Bill originating in an armed rival of the Parliament was rejected could not be deplored by the friends of the liberties of Parliament; but that all reform bills should be steadily thrown out was ominous and disappointing. In 1785, in 1791, in 1793, and in 1794, Grattan and others brought forward measures of reform, but in vain.

The Regency Question, 1789.—In 1789 a collision took place between the Irish Parliament and the Parliament of Great Britain. George III. became insane, and a regent had to be appointed. Two parties were formed in England on this question—one, under Pitt, wished to grant limited powers to the Prince of Wales as regent; the other, under Fox, to make the Prince regent with full kingly power. The Irish Parliament espoused Fox's view, and took the initiative in the matter. The affair did not become serious, as the King recovered speedily; but it was of importance as showing that there was nothing to prevent the nomination of two regents—one in Ireland one in England, and that that and other complications arising from the existence of an Independent Irish Parliament were unbearable, and were only to be cured by a complete Union. This at any rate was the English view of the matter.

Catholic Emancipation.—The second object of all Irish patriots during the years of the Independent Parliament was Catholic Emancipation. For long it was the enlightened among the Protestants alone who openly sought this; the Catholics themselves were too downtrodden to speak up. An institution called the Catholic Committee had existed for some years. Its avowed object was to watch over the interests of Catholics; but it did not dare to do much.

The United Irishmen, 1791.—In 1791 a society calling itself The United Irishmen was formed by Wolfe Tone and others, for the purpose of obtaining the two things needed for Ireland—Parliamentary Reform and Catholic Emancipation. This society took its rise in Belfast, and its adherents were the Presbyterians of the North, who most of all Irishmen had been influenced by the ideas of the French Revolution. Tone, who was a far-sighted man, sought to make this society in reality a Society of United Irishmen, and strove to bring into its ranks the Catholics of Dublin and the South. He therefore sought for the co-operation of Keogh, a rich and enlightened Dublin merchant, and a leading spirit in the Catholic Committee. Keogh was followed by the greater number of the Catholic Committee. He and his supporters were for demanding the franchise for their co-religionists. The aristocratic and priestly element of the committee, headed by Lord Kenmare, hung back, determining to wait on Providence and the Protestant majority rather than to cast in their lot with a society which numbered many Republicans, and even some Separatists. Notwithstanding this division in their ranks, the United Irishmen grew and flourished, and became a great power in the land—the hope of the patriots and the dread of the government. A great gulf was fixed between the executive government and all who desired reform in Ireland. The whole evil spirit of the government was embodied in the Earl of Clare—"Black Jack Fitzgibbon." The aim of this minister was to keep alive for ever the religious feuds which desolated Ireland, and to keep the Cabinets of England from all action which might tend to conciliate Ireland. He brought to pass one thing which he did not wish. It was mainly through his vehement opposition that Wolfe Tone was able to rouse the Catholics throughout the land to a sense of their wrongs and their rights, and to urge them to demand justice.

Lord Clare rouses the Catholics, 1792.—A plan was formed that a Catholic Convention, composed of representatives from all parts of Ireland, should meet in Dublin. Lord Clare moved heaven and earth to prevent the assembling of this Convention. From every corner of Ireland he stirred up a furious outcry against the independence of the Catholics, and his efforts did more by a great deal than he had intended. He roused indeed the Protestant wrath, and that wrath goaded the longsuffering Catholic to shake off his lethargy. "Lord Clare," said Keogh, "has done what I so long attempted, and attempted in vain—he has roused the Catholics."

The Catholic Convention, 1792.—The Catholic Convention met in Dublin on the 3rd of December, 1792. A petition to the King, praying for the complete enfranchisement of the Catholics, was drawn up. Five delegates, among whom was Keogh, took it to London, where it was graciously received by George III., who promised to recommend the Catholic cause to the Irish Parliament. In the next session of Parliament (1793) a bill was passed which, by giving a vote to all 40s. freeholders, enabled Catholics to vote in elections; but the amendment which would have rendered the bill of use, a clause allowing Catholics to sit in Parliament, was thrown out. Undaunted, the party of reform pressed on, at first with somewhat faint success; for the fortune of Ireland depended on the exigencies of English party politics.

Lord Fitzwilliam Lord-Lieutenant, 1794.—In the end of 1794 a favourable turn of affairs gave Ireland a good Viceroy—Lord Fitzwilliam, a friend of Grattan and of Catholic Emancipation. Grattan was very hopeful; for Pitt had said to him that he had counselled the new Viceroy not to bring forward emancipation as a government measure, but if Government were pressed to yield to it. The secret injunction of the Prime Minister was not known, but it was divined from the sending of Fitzwilliam. Loud and hearty welcome greeted the new Viceroy, and petitions for Catholic Emancipation poured in from every quarter. Parliament met; large and liberal supplies were voted, and Grattan prepared, in concert with the Viceroy, a bill granting full emancipation to the Catholics. A Reform Bill was to follow. The Irish were tempted to hope that now at last the wrongs of ages seemed about to be righted. This patriotic delusion did not last long.

The King declares himself against Catholic Emancipation.—The King suddenly and stoutly declared himself to be against Catholic Emancipation, and considerations of party and power overrode all else in the mind of Pitt. Fitzwilliam was suddenly recalled, and all the hope of Ireland went with him. Corrupt and powerless for good, the Irish Parliament dragged on. Grattan made many noble efforts for reform, but all in vain. At length, in despair of the public weal, he resigned his seat in Parliament, and retired into the country.

CHAPTER IX.

THE REBELLION OF 1798. *THE UNION.*

Suppression of the United Irishmen—With the downfall of all hope of constitutional redress of wrongs, the counsels of the disloyal prevailed, disaffection was rife, and outrage filled the land. The Society of United Irishmen, being judged treasonable, was suppressed by the government; but it only disappeared from the sight of men to take deep root as a secret society. The aim of the first United Irishmen had been to obtain Parliamentary reform, and as a means to that end Catholic Emancipation. The aim of the United Irishmen, when reconstituted as a secret society, was to break loose from England, and to make Ireland into a Republic. This could only be done by foreign aid. Tone went to America, and thence to France, to solicit this aid.

Formation of Orange Lodges, 1795.—In the meantime a society arose in the opposite camp of the Irish. The Protestants of the North formed themselves into Orange Lodges, called after the prince of "glorious, pious, and immortal memory." The aim of the Orangemen, who grew and multiplied, was to drive all Catholics from Ulster. In pursuit of this aim no atrocity seemed to them too great to permit. Law was of no avail in Ulster. Troops were sent down to quell the

Orangemen, but their success was not great. The turmoil of the Orangemen in the North was rivalled by the turmoil of the Defenders in the West. Lord Carhampton was sent to restore order, and he and those under him could only support the law by breaking the law. It was found necessary to pass an Indemnity Bill to screen these high-handed supporters of law and order. A Coercion Act of tremendous force was passed in order to keep down the excited country. This Coercion Act thrust the evil underground, but the evil remained.

Hoche's Expedition, 1796.—The foreign aid was what all waited for. Tone's efforts were successful. In December, 1796, a French fleet, bearing 15,000 soldiers, well armed, and provided with arms for the Irish, set sail under General Hoche for the invasion of Ireland. The English squadron, which should have barred the way, did nothing, and Hoche and his men sailed on towards Ireland, which lay defenceless; but the elements did the work which the English ships neglected. A sea fog came down on the fleet, and the ships parted company, and struggled separately on their way. On the morning of the 22nd of December the fleet found itself in clear weather again off the Irish coast; but seven ships were missing, and among them the *Fraternité*, which bore General Hoche. Nothing could be done without the general. As they waited for him a furious storm from the east arose, which made the landing of the French impossible. For six days the storm raged, and several ships were destroyed. At last those ships that remained struggled back to France, and so ended another luckless Irish attempt to throw off the English yoke by foreign aid.

Planning of the Rebellion.—In despair the United Irishmen determined to attempt an unaided rising—a misguided and hopeless undertaking. Grattan was throughout opposed to violent measures. He lent no countenance to the project of revolt, but he urged unceasingly on the Government the necessity of concession to reasonable popular demands. The Government, however, preferred to encounter the rising disloyalty with mere repression. The number of informers has always been a marked feature in the history of Irish conspiracy. At this time they swarmed, and every word and action of the conspirators was brought in to the Government by the army of spies. The arrest of some of the leaders of the conspiracy hastened the movements of those left at liberty. Lord Edward Fitzgerald, lying hidden in Dublin, was the soul of the plot. The rising was fixed for the 23rd of May, 1798. It was planned to seize the capital, the Viceroy, and the Privy Council. The arrangements were known to the Government, and measures were accordingly taken.

Arrest of Lord Edward Fitzgerald.—A few days before the 23rd Lord Edward Fitzgerald was betrayed in his hiding-place. He resisted the soldiers sent to capture him; a desperate fight took place, and Lord Edward was arrested, though he died shortly afterwards of the wounds he received. His arrest was followed by the capture of the other leaders of the conspiracy, and Dublin was saved. Martial law was proclaimed in the city, and a strong military force preserved order.

Local Risings.—In the country places there were many abortive risings. Scattered bodies of rebels contended with scattered bodies of soldiery, and where

they fought the luckless inhabitants suffered. Riot
and bloodshed prevailed; but one place was isolated
from another, and the soldiery won the day. In a
week the rioting at large was over, but all the strength
and all the horror of the rebellion was concentrated in
one county, and it is the war of Wexford which
marks the year '98 with so hideous a stain.

The War of Wexford.—Wexford had only recently
become a seat of disaffection. For many years it had
been one of the quietest and least discontented spots in
Ireland; but the general tyranny and lawless oppression
whereby the English troops and the Irish yeomanry
sought to maintain the law and to avert civil war, did
its work, and Wexford rose. On the 27th of May a
disorderly host of men and women, some thousands in
number, and led by a priest, Father John Murphy,
defeated and destroyed a small body of militia sent
against them, rushed upon Ferns, and burnt the bishop's
palace. Then, driving before them herds of infuriated
cattle, they marched upon Enniscorthy, which they
attacked. After a gallant resistance the garrison fled
out to Wexford, leaving the rebels in possession.
Wexford was next to be seized. The soldiers, finding
themselves too few for adequate defence of the town,
marched away. The rebels set up a kind of government
in Wexford, and chose as their leader Bagenal
Harvey.

The Camp of Vinegar Hill.—Father John Murphy
had set up a great camp at Vinegar Hill, near Enniscorthy,
and thither congregated masses of the lowest
of the people—men and women. Throughout the
county the rebels had it their own way. Two places
only were held by the king's forces—Duncannon and

New Ross. Bagenal Harvey determined to attack New Ross, and advanced at the head of 30,000 rebels against the town, defended by a force of under 1400 men. The conflict was desperate, but discipline won the day. After ten hours' fighting the rebels gave way; but the end of that day witnessed a dreadful deed. One of the retreating rebels ran to a place called Scullabogue, where over 200 loyalists lay imprisoned in a house and a barn. The fugitive announced that he bore an order from Bagenal Harvey to the effect that all these prisoners were to die. Accordingly the prisoners in the house were piked, and the barn was fired, being filled with 184 persons, who died from suffocation and burning. Harvey was horrified at this crime done in his name. He quarrelled with his men on the matter, and gave up the command to Father Philip Roche, a burly priest.

Troops poured into Wexford, but did not at once succeed in putting down the rebellion. For a time there was a panic that Dublin was again in danger; but the rebels had no general worthy the name, and they wasted their time in plundering at large, and did not attempt to march on Dublin. On the 9th of June there was a repetition of the day of New Ross. Again 30,000 of the rebels marched upon a small force of the king's troops, this time shut up in Arklow, the key of the Dublin road. After a day's hard fighting the rebels, deprived of their captain, withdrew defeated. This defeat put an end to all bold schemes. The insurgents remained encamped in their two strongholds on the hill of Lacken, and on Vinegar Hill. The latter camp had a monopoly of atrocities. The followers of Father John Murphy brought into the camp all the loyal

Protestants they could find; these luckless prisoners were shut up in a windmill, and then put to death. Four hundred in all perished in this slaughter.

Capture of Vinegar Hill.—It was impossible for the force stationed in Ireland to put down this rebellion. Eight thousand men were sent from England; 7000 more joined them, and a well-armed force, with General Lake as commander-in-chief, set out into Wexford. The Englishmen surrounded Vinegar Hill. The rebel forces nearly equalled their antagonists in number, but they had not much ammunition, and no discipline or strategy. The result was what might have been expected. After fierce fighting the rebels abandoned their hill, and fled away to the south, towards Wexford, where a scene of horror was being acted. General Lake had sent a force to attack Wexford; this force met with Father Roche and his men, who had abandoned the hill of Lacken. A battle took place which had no decisive ending. Father Roche fell short of ammunition, and withdrew in good order to a strong position without the walls. Then the populace of Wexford began to wreak their vengeance on all the Protestants within their reach. These unhappy victims were dragged to the middle of the bridge where a mock trial was held, and they were murdered one by one to the number of ninety-seven, and flung into the river. The rumour of defeat, and of the approach of the enemy, cut short the murderous work. The insurgent troops fled away into the mountains, dispersed, and in course of time disappeared. Wexford was given up to the mercy of the soldiers; and they, remembering the barn of Scullabogue, and the bridge of Wexford, had no mercy, and dealt death and destruction throughout the county. Bagenal Harvey, Father Philip Roche, and many others, were hung upon the bridge at Wexford. Father John Murphy was executed elsewhere. Martial law prevailed, and frequently enough it degenerated into mere lynch-law and the wanton burning of homesteads.

Lord Cornwallis lands in Ireland.—The rebellion having lost all semblance of danger, it was deemed desirable to set up in Ireland a Viceroy who should not be so cold and merciless as Lord Camden. Lord Cornwallis was sent over to act both as Viceroy and Commander-in-Chief. Lord Castlereagh accompanied him as Chief Secretary. The new Viceroy, who strove to be just and temperate, was deeply distressed at the state of feeling he found amongst the English in Ireland. He says in a letter, "The conversation of the principal persons of the country all tends to encourage the system of blood; and the conversation even at my table, where you will suppose I do all I can to prevent it, always turns on hanging, shooting, burning, &c.; and if a priest has been put to death the greatest joy is expressed by the whole company. So much for Ireland and my wretched situation."

He issued a proclamation, "promising protection to all insurgents guilty of rebellion only, who should surrender their arms and take the Oath of Allegiance." He carried an Amnesty Bill, and enforced strict discipline on the army, whilst he showed kindness to the unhappy people. A few of the leading conspirators who had been captured were hung, and the rest were banished for life. Two ridiculous and unsuccessful French expeditions disturbed the West of Ireland. On board one of the unlucky French ships was Wolfe

Tone, the founder of the United Irishmen. He was captured, tried, and condemned to death; but he cut his throat, and died in prison.

The Union, 1800.—In the exhausted state of Ireland after the rebellion and its suppression, Pitt saw a favourable opportunity for bringing about the Union which he had so long planned. An overwhelming majority of the people of Ireland were bitterly opposed to any such measure, and the bill for effecting a Union was thrown out in the session of 1799; but by scattering abroad money and false hopes the Viceroy, his Chief Secretary, and the Lord Chancellor, won over votes to their side. A million and a half of money, and titles and places innumerable secured a bare majority in the House for the government measure. The mass of the Catholics throughout the country, awakened by Lord Clare from their long sleep, and persistently clamorous for their rights, were hushed into silence for the time by the promise that the Union once passed should be followed by their emancipation. The three men who brought about the Union looked upon their preparatory measures with very different eyes. Lord Cornwallis said, "My occupation is now of the most unpleasant nature, negotiating and jobbing with the most corrupt people under heaven. I despise and hate myself every hour for engaging in such dirty work, and am supported only by the reflection that without an Union the British Empire must be dissolved." Lord Castlereagh does not seem to have been disturbed in his mind by any such scruples; and Lord Clare, always glad to coerce his "damnable country," was quite happy. In May, 1800, the Irish Parliament passed the Act of Union, and decreed its own destruction. Grattan, in a splendid speech, lifted up his voice against the bill, but in vain.

The Act of Union decreed that the Irish Parliament should cease to exist, and that Ireland should be represented in the Imperial Parliament by one hundred members in the Commons House, and by four lords spiritual sitting in rotation, and twenty-eight lords temporal elective. It was further provided that the Irish Church should continue as then established, and that free trade should exist between England and Ireland.

CHAPTER X.

IRELAND IN THE NINETEENTH CENTURY.

The Four Grievances of Ireland.—The Union was meant to be the great panacea for all the woes of Ireland. It is true that it put an end to many troublesome questions, and that it gave one great boon to the Irish—free trade with England. But Ireland remained oppressed by many and great grievances, the four chief ones being the political slavery of the Catholics, the heavy burden of the tithes, the existence of the alien Church, and the system of land tenure. The agrarian grievances of Ireland, and the various attempts that have been made from time to time to remove them, must be treated apart. As to the three first grievances, it is the glory of the nineteenth century to have redressed them; and if it is objected that no far-seeing and benevolent legislation has done these things, and that Irish reforms have never been carried when they could possibly be deferred, it ought also to be remembered that the same reproach in a lesser degree may be levelled at all English reforms.

Catholic Emancipation.—The great body of Irish Catholics, so long inert and timid, had been stirred into active life in the times of the United Irishmen. The year 1793 granted them the electoral franchise;

but more than a generation passed away before their emancipation was completed, before Catholics were allowed to sit in Parliament. In the negotiations which preceded the Act of Union, the Irish Catholics were given to understand that their complete emancipation should speedily follow the Union. Bribed by this brilliant prospect, they held their peace, and abstained from any organised opposition to the measure. The Union once accomplished, they were undeceived. The King's views on the question were no longer concealed by anxious ministers from the world at large. What those views were may best be explained in the King's own words : "My inclination to the Union with Ireland was chiefly founded on a trust that the uniting of the Established Churches of the two kingdoms would for ever shut the door to any further measures with respect to the Roman Catholics." So said King George III., and Pitt only escaped from the condemnation he deserved by posing as the unwilling victim of the royal obstinacy. Anger at the ministerial trick rolled through Ireland; but anger was unavailing, the Union was accomplished. All the wit of Ireland then set to work to get the boon which had been promised and withheld. The rebellion of Emmett does not enter into the history of the struggle for Catholic Emancipation; it was a mere survival of 1798.

Daniel O'Connell.—A new hero arose in Ireland in the beginning of this century—Daniel O'Connell, known as The Agitator. The old idol of the Irish Parliament, the patriot Henry Grattan, spent the last years of his life in advocating in the Parliament of Great Britain the claims of the Irish Catholics; but he died before success was won. The man who freed the Catholics was Daniel O'Connell. O'Connell was a barrister, eloquent and ambitious, clear in aim and strong in act. At the time of the Union he was only twenty-five years old, but he had already made his mark. The Union he hated and abhorred, and he very soon made up his mind as to what he wanted. He wished that the Union should be repealed, the Protestant Church deprived of its ascendancy, and that Catholics and Protestants, free alike, should sit in a Parliament in Dublin. To bring about this state of things he saw that it was necessary to stir up the great body of the Irish Catholics to demand their rights. The best way to reach the Catholics was through the priests. O'Connell set himself to make the priests do the work, and they did it. The struggle lasted for many years. What was called the Veto question delayed matters. The English Government offered to give emancipation to the Catholics on condition of having a right of veto on the appointment of Catholic prelates. More than once Irish opinion inclined to accept this compromise; but O'Connell, fearing loss of power to his Church, swayed it otherwise.

In 1824 O'Connell founded the Catholic Association, to be worked by the priests in every parish in Ireland, for divers avowed objects, the real object being to agitate in favour of emancipation. Vast sums of money were raised in order to carry on the agitation. This was called the Catholic Rent. The priests throughout the land exercised their enormous influence; O'Connell and his colleague, Richard Lalor Sheil, traversed the country and roused it. The Catholic Association came athwart the Government in every election. In 1828 O'Connell himself, though a Catholic, was returned for

Clare. The will of the whole people was now strung up, and as in 1782 it was irresistible. Catholic Emancipation was wrung from the ministry of the Duke of Wellington, in the year 1829, by the fear of civil war. As usual the gift was robbed of its grace. The 40s. freeholders, whose votes had done so much towards enfranchising their fellow-Catholics, were disfranchised lest they should do any further mischief. The Catholic Association was suppressed by law. O'Connell himself was refused admission to Parliament until he had been re-elected, on the ground that he had been elected while he was ineligible. All constitutional agitation was suppressed by the power given to the Viceroy to stop any public meeting which he deemed dangerous. Constitutional means of agitation being denied to Ireland, the old evil of the secret societies was intensified. Outrage was rife; coercion was the only remedy approved by the Executive, and the miserable circle of agitation and coercion began to revolve again.

Tithe Commutation Act, 1838.—The reform of English Parliamentary representation in 1832 was not without its influence on Irish legislation, though after the Reform Bill was passed, as before it, England rarely conceded anything to Irish demands except in response to increasing turbulence and intolerable agitation. In 1838 the Tithe Commutation Act was passed after a long and desperate struggle, in which the Irish were again led by O'Connell. An absolute and dogged refusal on the part of the tithe-payers to pay any tithe at all brought about the Act. The Catholic peasantry were released from the payment of tithes, and the Protestant landlords were required to pay instead.

Education.—Education demanded early attention. After the Union the conscientious among the Protestants felt uneasy at the thought of the mass of ignorant Catholics, doomed to ignorance as long as they remained faithful to their religion. An effort was accordingly made to educate without proselytizing, and a Society called the Kildare Street Society was formed in 1811, which established mixed schools for Catholics and Protestants. In these schools a secular education was given, and the Bible was read without note or comment. The British Parliament adopted as its basis the system thus established; and this system, extended and modified by measures passed in 1832 and subsequent years, still furnishes all classes in Ireland, who choose to avail themselves of it, with a sound secular training. The same liberal policy was adopted with respect to the College of Maynooth, originally founded during the French war for the education of the Irish priests. Sir Robert Peel gave it a permanent endowment in 1845, and at the same time established the three Queen's Colleges in Belfast, Cork, and Galway, often described as the Godless Colleges, because they provided an entirely unsectarian education. The Maynooth grant was frequently attacked by ultra Protestants in the English Parliament. Together with the *Regium Donum*—a grant made from the Imperial Exchequer towards the maintenance of the Presbyterian establishment in Ulster—the Maynooth grant was cancelled in 1868, by provisions in the Act whereby the Protestant Church in Ireland was finally disestablished and disendowed.

Repeal Agitation.—The Tithe Commutation Act

was deemed insufficient by O'Connell. Persuaded that the mind of England was bent on recalling or nullifying the freedom gained in 1829, the great agitator began to devote the whole of his strength to the task of rousing his countrymen to demand the repeal of the Union. He held monster meetings throughout the length and breadth of Ireland, as remarkable for their decency and order as for their burning enthusiasm; Father Matthew, the temperance priest, worked with him. The great year of the agitation was 1843. In the autumn of that year it reached such a height that the Government in alarm forbade the meetings, and tried O'Connell and some others on a charge of conspiracy. O'Connell was found guilty and sent to prison; but an appeal was made to the House of Lords, the Irish sentence was reversed, and O'Connell was freed after some months' imprisonment. This interlude had broken the back of the agitation. The personal power of the leader being for a time in abeyance the concord of the agitators was disturbed. The Young Irelanders were an offshoot of O'Connell's Repealers; the chief of them were Smith O'Brien, John Mitchel, T. F. Meagher, John Dillon, and Charles Gavan Duffy.

The Potato Famine.—In 1846 the potato crop failed in Ireland, and a dreadful famine ensued, which embittered and intensified all the questions at issue between England and Ireland. Thousands died from starvation, and emigration removed as many more; so that ten years after the famine broke out the total population of Ireland had been reduced by more than a million. Strenuous attempts were made by the Government and people of England to relieve the distress caused by the famine, but its intensity served nevertheless to increase the perennial discontent of the Irish peasantry. The year 1848—a period of revolution throughout Europe—was one of universal ferment in Ireland. The party of Young Ireland very nearly succeeded in stirring up a revolt; but the rising was mismanaged, its leaders were unready, and hostilities began and ended with the defeat and arrest of Smith O'Brien, and one or two of his associates, in a cabbage garden at Ballingarry, in Tipperary.

The Fenian Conspiracy.—The rising of 1848 was crushed, but discontent and disaffection could not be crushed. A steady stream of Irish emigrants sought the New World, and the saying of Grattan began to be fulfilled—" Whatever is bold and disconsolate . . . to that point will precipitate, and what you trample on in Europe will sting you in America." The Fenian conspiracy of 1867 was but the latest outcome of that network of secret societies which for generations has undermined Ireland. In 1867 and 1868 Fenian outrages and menaces were rife in England. These culminated in a cowardly attempt to rescue certain prisoners detained in Clerkenwell Gaol by means of an explosion, which caused great suffering and loss of life.

Disestablishment of the Irish Church, 1867.—In 1867 Mr. Gladstone, as leader of the Liberal party, had carried in the House of Commons a resolution in favour of the disestablishment of the Irish Church. In the autumn of the same year a dissolution of Parliament resulted in the return of a large Liberal majority. Mr. Disraeli, the Tory Premier, resigned, and was replaced by Mr. Gladstone. One of the first measures of the new Government was a bill for the disestablishment and disendowment of the Irish Church. This was carried, and was followed by the Land Act of 1870. In 1873 Mr. Gladstone attempted to deal with the question of education, the third branch, as he called it, of the upas-tree of Protestant ascendancy in Ireland. In this attempt he was unsuccessful, and the return of Mr. Disraeli to power in 1874 suspended for several years the operation and development of his rival's policy in Ireland. To which of the two policies, that of the Tories or that of the Liberals, is to be attributed the condition in which Ireland was found in 1880, when Mr. Gladstone returned to power, is a question which need not be decided here. It must suffice to say that once more in 1880 it became necessary for Parliament to take up that question of land tenure which from time immemorial had alienated Ireland from England, and had perplexed the legislatures and embarrassed the statesmen of both countries.

The Land Question.—The Act of 1793, which gave the Parliamentary franchise to all 40s. freeholders, resulted in a large increase of the number of small holdings. The Act of 1829 deprived the 40s. freeholders of their votes. In consequence, the landlords, being no longer induced to cut up their holdings in order to multiply votes, inclined towards consolidation, and eviction was rife. Famine and poverty were the portion of the small tenants who remained, and the wretched system of land tenure which obtained in Ireland threatened to make famine and poverty perennial. The inextricable confusion which came from the superposition, never willingly accepted by the people, of the feudal system upon the tribal system, has more than once been mentioned. The many wholesale confiscations—the original Conquest of Henry II., the Plantations of Elizabeth and James I., and the Cromwellian settlement—had made the confusion worse. Absentee landlords, the growth of a bad feeling between them and their tenants, and the mischievous system whereby the tenant repaired and improved, and the landlord secured the ultimate advantage, have kept up the misery to this day. Ulster was in some respects an exception to the general distress and discontent; for there the system of rack-rent was modified and softened by the custom known as the Ulster tenant right. This custom, which arose, as we have shown, in the years following the Ulster Plantation, gave the tenant permissive fixity of tenure, accompanied by the right to sell the goodwill of his farm. When it is remembered that by the opposition of England to the growth of trade and manufacture the people of Ireland have had no means of gaining subsistence save from the land, the terrible and lasting misery resulting from the evil system of land tenure may be understood.

Affairs in Ireland grew steadily worse from 1829 onwards. The measure known as the Catholic Emancipation Act, while it grudgingly gave permission to Catholics to sit in Parliament, did not alter the system of patronage whereby all the chief offices were filled by Protestants; and by disfranchising the 40s. freeholders, it condemned to political death by far the largest class of Catholic voters in the land. All this weighed on the mind and spirit of the people, and increased the material misery.

The Devon Commission, 1842.—The first serious

attempt at agrarian reform was made in the year 1835 by Mr. Sharman Crawford, member for Dundalk, who brought in a bill to improve the condition of the Irish tenant. The main purpose of this bill was that the tenant should be entitled, in the case of his eviction, to compensation for permanent improvements made with the landlord's consent. This bill was brought in in 1835 and 1836, but met with violent opposition, and was thrown out. Seven years afterwards Mr. Crawford succeeded in obtaining the appointment of a Royal Commission to investigate the "occupation of land in Ireland." This Commission, known from its chairman, Lord Devon, as the Devon Commission, marks a great epoch in the Irish land question. The Commissioners, in their Report, brought out strongly the facts that great misery existed in Ireland, and that the cause of the misery was the system of land tenure. The following extract from the Report indicates the general nature of its conclusions: "A reference to the evidence of most of the witnesses will show that the agricultural labourer of Ireland continues to suffer the greatest privations and hardships; that he continues to depend upon casual and precarious employment for subsistence; that he is badly housed, badly fed, badly clothed, and badly paid for his labour. Our personal experience and observations during our enquiry have afforded us a melancholy confirmation of these statements, and we cannot forbear expressing our strong sense of the patient endurance which the labouring classes have generally exhibited under sufferings greater, we believe, than the people of any other country in Europe have to sustain." And the remedy for the evil is to be found, continues the Report, in "an increased and improved cultivation of the soil," to be gained by securing for the tenant "fair remuneration for the outlay of his capital and labour."

Various Attempts at Land Reform.—No sooner was this Report issued than great numbers of petitions were presented to the House of Lords, and supported by Lord Devon, praying for legislative reform of the land evils; and in June, 1845, a bill was introduced into the House of Lords by Lord Stanley, on behalf of the government of Sir Robert Peel, for "the purpose of providing compensation to tenants in Ireland, in certain cases, on being dispossessed of their holdings, for such improvements as they may have made during their tenancy." By the selfish opposition of the Irish landlords this bill was thrown out. Two days after its rejection in the House of Lords Mr. Sharman Crawford brought into the House of Commons a Tenant Right Bill, and met with as little success. In 1846 a government bill was introduced, bearing a strong resemblance to that of Lord Stanley; but the ministry was overthrown, and the bill was dropped. A Liberal ministry under Lord John Russell came into power in July, 1846, and Irish hopes again began to rise.

In 1847 the indefatigable Mr. Crawford brought in a bill, whose purpose was to extend the Ulster custom to the whole of Ireland; it was thrown out. A well-meant but in the end unsuccessful attempt to relieve the burdens of embarrassed landlords without redressing the grievances of rack-rented tenants, was made in 1848 by the measure well known as the Encumbered Estates Act. This Act had for its object to restore capital to the land; but with capital it brought in a class of proprietors who lacked the virtues as well as the vices of their predecessors, and were even more oppressive to the tenantry.

Between 1847 and 1860 innumerable bills were introduced and disappeared. In 1860 an Act passed by Lord Palmerston's government attempted to deal with Irish agrarian discontent by declaring the relation between landlord and tenant to be one of contract, and not of tenure. This Act proved to be almost a dead letter. It was found impossible to extinguish Irish ideas of tenure by the mere letter of an Act of Parliament, and matters consequently went from bad to worse. In 1870 the policy attempted in 1860 was reversed. Mr. Gladstone passed an Act, of which the main purposes were:

1. To obtain for the tenants in Ireland security of tenure.

2. To encourage the making of improvements throughout the country.

3. To create a peasant proprietorship in Ireland.

This Act was inadequate in that it secured to the tenant the value of his improvements only in case of eviction, whereas the one desire of the tenant was to retain his holding. Hence distress and discontent continued, and in 1879 and 1880 were almost fanned into insurrection by a partial failure of the harvest, and by the influence of a powerful and unscrupulous organization known as the Land League. Another Commission, under the presidency of Lord Bessborough, was appointed by the government of Mr. Gladstone in 1880. Early in 1881 it reported, and the result of its report was the Land Act of 1881, whereby the system of land tenure, known as the "Three F's"—fixity of tenure, fair rent, and free sale—was established, and provision was incidentally made for emigration on the one hand, and for the purchase of their holdings by occupying tenants on the other.

This great reform is now in full operation throughout Ireland. Its final results cannot as yet be foreseen, but it bids fair to allay agrarian discontent; and if it should succeed in doing so it may yet come to be regarded as the charter of peace between the two countries.

INDEX

	Page		Page
Abjuration, Oath of	85	Bolingbroke	20
Absentees, Law against	17	Boulter, Primate	89, 91
Absentees, Tax on	98	Boyne, Battle of the	80, 81
Account, Commissioners of	98	Brehon Laws	3, 53
Act of Renunciation	110	Brian, King	5
Address, The American	99	Brotherhood of St. George	20
Allegiance, Oath of	85, 122	Bruce, Edward	14
Amnesty Bill	122	Bruce, Robert	14–16
Antrim	28, 34–36	Buckingham, Lord	103, 105
Aquila, Don Juan de	50	Bull, Adrian IV.'s	6
Ardscull	15	Burghley, Lord	39
Arklow	120	Burgo, William de	11
Armagh	48, 57	Burgo, De, The "Red	
Armagh, Synod of	8	Earl"	15
Athlone	82	Burkes, The	38
Attainder, Act of	78	Burke, Edmund	99
Aughrim, Battle of	82	Burke, Gervase	105
Augmentation Act	96		
Avaux, Count of	76, 79	Camden, Lord	122
		Carew, Sir George	49, 51
Bacon, Lord	21, 58	Carhampton, Lord	117
Bagnal, Sir Henry	48	Carlisle, Lord	105
Baker, Major	77	Carlow	71
Ballingarry	131	Carrickfergus	15, 78, 80
Baltinglass, Lord	43	Carrigafoyle, Castle of	39
Belfast	112, 129	Carteret, Lord Granville	91
Bellingham, Sir Edward	26, 27	Castle of the Island	39
Bessborough Commission	136	Castle Chamber	54, 62
Bessborough, Lord	136	Castle Connell	24
Birmingham, Jean de	16	Castlereagh, Lord	122, 123
Blackwater Town	48	Catholics in Ireland, 34, 50, 54,	
Bloods, The Five	12	60, 63, 64, 69, 70, 75, 86–88,	
Blount, Charles, Lord		95, 100, 101, 105, 106, 108,	
Mountjoy	49, 51–53	112–114, 116, 123, 125–127,	
Boisselot	81	129, 133.	

INDEX.

Catholic Association of 1759, 101	Davis, Sir John 58, 60, 61
Catholic Association of 1824 ... 127, 128	Declaration of Independence, The Irish 104, 107
Catholic Committee ... 112	Defenders, The ... 117
Catholic Convention 113, 114	Dermot Mac Murrough... 7
Catholic Emancipation, 109, 111, 112, 114–116, 125, 126–128, 133.	Derry 33, 58, 76–78
	Desmonds, The ... 39, 41
	Desmond, Earls of, 18, 24, 25, 38–41, 43.
Catholic Rent 127	
Cavan 57	Desmond Rebellion, 35, 38–42
Chandeboy 35	Desmond, Sir James of 41
Charlemont ... 67, 79	Desmond, Sir John of 40, 41
Charlemont, Lord 102, 106	Devon Commission 133, 134
Charles I. ... 62, 66	Devon, Lord ... 134, 135
Charles II. ... 75, 78, 83	Dillon, John 130
Chatham, Lord ... 98	Dingle Harbour... ... 37
Chesterfield, Lord ` ... 91	Disraeli, Mr. ... 131, 132
Chichester, Sir Arthur 53–59	Dobbs, Francis 106
Chichester, Lord ... 67	Don Bastian de San Josepho, 41
Christianity, Introduction of 3	Donegal 57
Civita Vecchia 37	Down 28
Clare 62, 127	Drapier's Letters 90, 91
Clerkenwell Explosion ... 131	Drogheda 70
Clogheen 93	Drury, Sir William ... 38
Clontarf, Battle of ... 5	Dublin, 8–10, 19, 20, 23, 27, 32, 34, 36, 39, 48, 64, 68, 71, 72, 77–81, 107, 111–114, 118, 120, 127.
Clyn, John 15	
Coercion Acts ... 94, 117	
Cogan, Mylo de 11	
Coleraine ... 57, 58, 66	Dublin Castle 67
Commercial Legislation 87, 88	Duffy, Charles Gavan ... 130
Connaught, 11, 33, 37, 61, 62, 64, 65, 71, 72, 88.	Duncannon 119
	Dundalk, 15, 16, 31, 33, 80, 134
Connemara 38	Dungannon 67
Conquest, Anglo-Norman 6	Dungannon, Barons of, 28, 30, 44.
Cork 11, 39, 42, 82, 129	
Cork, County of 52, 71, 93	Dungannon, Convention of, 106
Cornwallis, Lord 122, 123	D'Usson 83
Counties, Ireland divided into, 6	
Counties Palatine ... 11	Eden, Sir W. 105
Courcy, John de ... 11	Edward VI. 26
Coyne and Livery ... 17	Elizabeth, 24, 28–32, 34–39, 42, 44, 46–49, 52, 133.
Crawford, Mr. Sharman, 134, 135	
Crofts, Sir James ... 27	Emmett 126
Cromwell, Oliver 70, 71	Encumbered Estates Act 135
Cromwellian Settlement, 71–74, 133.	Enniscorthy 119
	Enniskillen ... 76, 77

Enniskilleners, The ... 78
Essex, Walter Devereux, Earl of ... 35, 36
Essex, Robert Devereux, Earl of ... 48, 49
Eustace, James, Lord Baltinglass 40
Eva, Princess 8, 11
Everard, Sir John ... 60

Faughared, J. 16
Fenian Conspiracy ... 131
Fermanagh 57
Ferns 119
Fitz-Aldelm 11
Fitzgerald, Gerald 25, 28
Fitzgerald, Lord Edward 118
Fitzgibbon, John, Earl of Clare ... 113, 123
Fitzmaurice, Sir James 37, 38
Fitz-Stephen, Robert 7, 8, 11
Fitzwilliam, Sir William, 29, 30, 44.
Fitzwilliam, Lord 114, 115
Flood, Henry, 98, 99, 106, 110, 111.
Fosterage ... 13, 17
Fox, Charles James 105, 111
Foyle, Lough 33
Fraternité 117

Galway 65, 81-83, 86, 129
Gavelkind 2
George I. 90
George II. 92
George III., 94, 95, 111, 114, 115, 126.
Geraldines, The, 8, 22, 23, 29, 38
Giants' Causeway ... 36
Ginkel, Baron ... 82, 83
Gladstone, Mr. 131, 132, 136
Glenmalure 40
Glynnes, The 36
Godless Colleges ... 129
Gossipred ... 13, 17
Graces, The 62-64

Grafton, Duke of ... 91
Grattan, Henry, 99, 101, 106-108, 110, 111, 114, 115, 118, 124, 126, 131.
Gray, Neil 30
Grey, Lady Elizabeth ... 23
Grey, Lord Leonard ...24-26
Grey de Wilton, Lord, 40, 41, 43

Habeas Corpus Act ... 105
Halifax, Lord ... 94, 95
Hamilton, Richard ... 77
Harcourt, Lord ... 98-100
Harrington, Lord ... 91
Harvey, Bagenal, 119, 120, 122
Henry II. 7-10, 65, 133
Henry VII. 21
Henry VIII. ... 23, 26, 28
Hely Hutchinson 96, 99
Hetherington, Edward ... 72
High Commission Court 64
Hoadley, Primate ... 89
Hoche, General ... 117

Indemnity Act 117
Irvine, Colonel 106

James I., 53, 54, 56-58, 60-62, 133.
James II. ... 75-81, 83
Jesuits, The 37
John, King 9

Kendal, Duchess of ... 90
Kenmare, Lord 113
Keogh, John ... 112, 113
Kerry :.. 37, 39, 52
Kildare 71
Kildare, Earls of, 18, 22, 24, 29, 40, 41.
Kildare Street Society ... 129
Kilkenny 39
Kilkenny, Statute of 13, 16
King's County 61
Kinsale 50, 51, 77, 82
Kinsale, Battle of ... 50

INDEX.

Lacken 120
Lacy, Hugh de ... 10, 11
Lake, General 121
Land Act of 1860 ... 136
Land Act of 1870 132, 136
Land Act of 1881 ... 136
Land League 136
Land System, 2, 125, 132, 133
La Touche, Mr. 103
Laud 64
Lauzun, Count 79-81
Leinster ... 10, 71, 88
Leinster, Duke of ... 102
Leinster, Plantations in 60
Leitrim 61
Limerick 25, 39, 81-83, 86
Limerick, County of ... 93
Limerick, Treaty of ... 83
Limerick, The Wood of 38
Linen Manufacture 66, 88
Lionel, Duke of Clarence 17
London, City of... 58, 65
Londonderry (see Derry).
Longford 61
Lords Justices, The 68, 69
Louis XIV. ... 75, 79, 81
Lucas, Charles 91
Lundy, Governor ... 77

M'Connells, The 28, 34
M'Murroughs, The ... 12
MacPhelim, Sir Brian ... 35
Malby, Sir Nicholas ... 38
Marlborough, Earl of ... 82
Mary, Queen 28
Matthew, Father ... 130
Maumont, Marshal ... 77
Maynooth, College of ... 129
Mayo ... 38, 65
Meagher, T. F. 130
Meath 6, 10
Mitchell, John 130
Money Bill ... 94, 97
Morgan, Major 73
Morocco 37
Morrison, Fynes ... 48

Mortimer, Lord Roger ... 19
Munster, 6, 24, 37, 38, 40, 42, 49, 71, 88.
Munster, Plantation of 43
Murphy, Father John, 119, 120, 122.
Mutiny Bill, Irish, 105, 107, 108.

Nenagh 93
Nesta, Princess 7
New Ross 120
Newry 67
North, Lord 107
Northumberland, Earl of 28

Oakboys, The 94
O'Briens, The 12
O'Brien, Prince of Thomond ... 24, 25
O'Brien's Bridge 24, 25
O'Brien, Smith ... 130, 131
O'Byrnes, The 61
O'Connell, Daniel, 126-128, 130
O'Connors, The... ... 12
Octennial Act 96
O'Donnells, The, 28, 29, 31, 33
O'Donnell, Red Hugh, 46, 49, 51
O'Donnell, Rory, Earl of
  Tyrconnel 55
O'Molaghlins, The ... 12
O'Neils, The ... 12, 25, 28
O'Neil, Con, Earl of
  Tyrone 28
O'Neil, Hugh, Earl of
  Tyrone 44-52, 55, 56
O'Neil, Shan 28-34, 37, 44
O'Neil, Turlough Luineach, 34, 44, 45.
Orangemen ... 116, 117
Ormond, Earls of 18, 25
Ormond, Duke of 38-41
Ostmen, The 5, 80

Pale, The, 14, 20, 28, 33, 40, 41, 68.

INDEX. 143

Palmerston, Lord ... 136
Parliament of England, 69, 70, 73, 85, 88, 110, 111.
Parliament of Great Britain and Ireland, 124, 128, 129, 131-137.
Parliament, The Long ... 69
Parliament of Ireland, 10, 17, 20, 21, 26, 59, 60, 63, 77, 78, 84-87, 92, 94-101, 103-105, 107-112, 114, 115, 123, 124
Parliamentary Reform, 109-112
Parsons, Sir William ... 61
Patriots, The 92
Peel, Sir Robert 129, 135
Pelham, Sir William 39, 42
Penal Laws, The ...85-87
Perrot, Sir John 43, 44, 62
Pery, Mr. 97
Philip III. of Spain ... 50
Pitt, William, 109, 111, 114, 115, 123, 126.
Pole, Cardinal ... 24, 25
Ponsonby, Mr. 96-98
Pope John XXII. ... 14
Pope Pius V. 34
Portland, Duke of ... 107
Portmore 48
Potato Famine 130
Poynings, Sir Edward ... 21
Poynings' Law, 21, 94, 97, 105, 107, 110.
Presidents, The... ... 37
Prince of Wales... ... 111
Protestants, Irish, 60, 76, 77, 85, 87, 88, 101, 112, 116, 121, 127, 129.
Protestant Church in Ireland, 26, 55, 64, 124-127, 129, 131, 132.

Queen's County 61

Raghlin, Massacre at ... 36
Raleigh, Walter 40, 41, 43
Ravenspur 20

Rebellion of 1641 67-70
Regency Question ... 111
Regium Donum ... 129
Repeal Agitation ... 129
Richard, Duke of York 21
Richard II. ... 17, 19, 20
Roche, Father Philip, 120-122
Rockingham, Lord ... 107
Roderic, King ... 8, 9, 11
Roscommon 65
Rosen, General 77
Roses, Wars of the ...20, 21
Russell, Lord John ... 135
Russell, Sir William ... 46

St. Leger, Sir Anthony, 25-27
St. Malachy 4
St. Patrick 4
St. Patrick, Cathedral of 81
St. Ruth ... 82, 83
Sanders, Nicolas ... 37
Sarsfield, Colonel Patrick, 82, 83.
Schomberg, Count Meinhard 80
Schomberg, General 78-81
Scots, The 67
Scots, The Hebridean, 28, 29, 34-36.
Scots, Queen of 32
Scullabogue ... 120, 121
Settlement of Henry II. 10
Settlers, Grants to the First ... 10, 11
Seven Years' War ... 92
Shannon, The 24, 71, 72
Shannon, Lord ... 96-98
Sheil, Richard Lalor ... 127
Shireland, Act to Reduce Ireland to 37
Sidney, Sir Henry 83, 44
"Silken Lord," The 23, 24
Simple Repeal Controversy, 110
Sixth of George I., 88, 107, 110.
Skeffington, Sir William 24

Sligo 65	Ulster, 11, 29, 30, 32, 33-35,
Smerwick ... 37, 38, 40	37, 44-46, 48, 49, 52, 62,
Smith, John 32	67-69, 71, 78, 80, 94, 116,
Smith, Sir Thomas 34, 35	129, 133.
Spenser, Edmund 40, 42, 43	Ulster Custom ... 59, 133, 135
Stanley, Lord 135	Ulster, Plantation of 57, 133
Steelboys, The 94	Undertakers, The 92, 95-97
Stewart, Mr. 106	Union, The, 109, 110, 112, 123
Stone, Primate 89, 91, 92	125-127, 129.
Strafford, Thomas Went-	Union, Act of 124
worth, Earl of 63-66, 88	United Irishmen, 112, 113, 116,
Strongbow 7-11	123, 125.
Stukely, Sir Thomas ... 37	
Supremacy, Act of ... 26	Veto Question 127
Supremacy, Oath of ... 62	Vinegar Hill ... 119-121
Surleyboy 36	Volunteers, The 102-107
Sussex, Lord 29, 30, 32	Volunteer Convention ... 111
Swift, Dean ... 89, 90, 91	Volunteer Reform Bill ... 111
Talbot, Richard, Earl of	Walker, George... ... 77
Tyrconnel ... 76, 81-83	Walpole, Sir Robert ... 90
Tanist 2	Waterford 8, 9, 19, 81
Tanistry 2	Waterford, County of ... 93
Tara Hill 25	Wellington, Duke of ... 128
Three F's 137	Wesley, John 93
Tipperary, County of 93, 131	Westmeath 6, 61
Tithes, The ... 89, 125	Wexford 8, 81, 119, 121, 122
Tithe Commutation Act, 89, 128,	Wexford, County of, 61, 119, 120
129.	Whiteboys, The 89, 93, 94
Tone, Wolfe, 112, 113, 116, 117,	Wicklow ... 61, 73
123.	William III., 75, 77, 78, 80-82
Tonragee 67	Winter, Sir William 39, 40
Tories, The 73	Wood's Halfpence 90-92
Townshend, Lord 95-98	Woollen Manufacture ... 66
Transubstantiation, Decla-	Wool Trade 87
ration against ... 85	
Tyrconnel 31	Yellow Ford, Battle of the 48
Tyrone, County of 34, 57	Yelverton 104
Tyrone, Captain of ... 31	Young Irelanders 130, 131

www.ingramcontent.com/pod-product-compliance
Lightning Source LLC
Chambersburg PA
CBHW030349170426
43202CB00010B/1311